Dr. Coleman is a thoughtful, charismatic and well-educated leader who has a passion for inclusion, resilience and diversity. Her message for women leaders is unique, timely and nuanced. This book provides well-researched considerations for women to tackle modern day leadership challenges.

– Ron Malhotra, bestselling author, entrepreneur, and founder of *The Successful Male*

THREE SECOND WORLD

Essentials for Engineering Your Future

DR. TANJIA COLEMAN

KMD BOOKS

First published in Australia in 2022
by KMD Books
Waikiki, WA 6169

Edited by Eleanor Narey
Typeset by Dylan Ingram
Proofread by Chelsea Wilcox

A catalogue record for this work is available from the National Library of Australia

National Library of Australia Catalogue-in-Publication data:

Three Second World/Tanjia Coleman

ISBN:
978-0-6456765-8-7
(Paperback)

This book is dedicated to my Mother, who consistently encourages me to dream big, be fearless, walk confidently, and never allow anyone to steal my joy. Writing this book would not have been possible without her unwavering support and encouragement.

CONTENTS

INTRODUCTION

This book is an eye-opener and also a guide that equips women of this century to know their space, their role, and the dos and don'ts of leadership, it also prepares and equips us for whatever leadership tasks lie ahead.

Women are gradually making their leadership presence felt in entrepreneurship, administration, education, engineering, health, etc. at regional, national, and global levels. Women are now resolved to break the traditional glass ceiling that barred them from entering leadership positions even if they possessed the requisite skills and talent to occupy them.

Resiliency and Reinvention have been how I've survived in business and throughout my life. What I learned early in life, is that nothing stays the same. You must be adaptable, nimble, and knowledgeable. I experienced tragic losses in my life at a young age and because of that, I don't stay in any situation that steals my joy. I will not allow that to happen. It doesn't matter if it's with an employer, leader, friend, or in a relationship, life is too short for any form of extended misery or one-sided sacrifice.

From my observations with many of the women I coach, I find

women doubt themselves because they are often seeking perfection. Their male counterparts will pass them by with 50% of what is required for a particular opportunity, while women continue to seek development to ensure they have 110% of attributes for the same opportunity.

WHAT IS LEADERSHIP?

Every organization needs a leader, irrespective of its size and functions. A leaderless organization is a "muddle of men and machine"; a country without leadership is anarchy; a society without leadership is a violent and dangerous place to live. Then, what is the meaning of leadership? What constitutes leadership?

A leader is a person who influences and encourages a group of people to work towards the realization of goals through empathy, understanding and kindess. The hallmark of leadership is the capacity to influence others towards accomplishing goals and towards betterment. An effective leader has an innate ability for connnecting people to their "why" and purpose. As Simon Sinek says, "It's those that start with why, that have the ability to inspire those around them or find others who inspire them."

Leadership is not gender-specific. It is a set of leadership qualities inherent or cultivated in a person or persons who develop themselves into great leaders with a mass following. Leaders can be either men or women. Leaders can only lead if they inspire others to follow.

Although leadership skills are acquired and shown by both men and women, certain differences exist in the basic traits and qualities possessed by men and women leaders. Although the leadership gap is improving and current research continues to demonstrate that men and women have distinctly different styles of leadership.

CHARACTERISTICS OF WOMEN LEADERSHIP

These are some common leadership styles of women leaders:

TRANSFORMATIONAL LEADERSHIP STYLE

Women leaders are more transformational leaders. They function as role models for their subordinates and they inspire their team through coaching. Great leaders emphasize teamwork and authentic communication as a key to successful outcomes. For most women leaders, leadership is not meant only for accomplishing organizational goals but for transforming their followers into better contributors to society.

EXECUTION AND STRATEGY FOCUSED

Women leaders are invariably focused on the completion of tasks assigned within deadlines. From an operational point, completing day-to-day tasks are necessary to ensure the smooth functioning of the company. Building strategic plans by which to execute is an essential competency of women leaders.

PREFER TO WORK IN A COLLEGIAL ATMOSPHERE

Women leaders generally prefer leading and creating flat organizational structures that enable all to work in a collegial atmosphere independently. A flat organizational structure overlooks the experience and knowledge of seasoned employees and the manager, women leaders are typically critical of the hierarchical structure of organizations.

PROMOTE COOPERATION AND COLLABORATION

To work in collaboration with others is a typical Theory Y characteristic. Women leaders promote cooperation and collaboration amongst team members. In this case, all the members of the team need to be clear of their roles and responsibilities, otherwise, it results in redundant work.

COMMUNICATION STYLE

Women leaders tend to be participatory and possess a democratic style of leading people. They seem to abhor the "command and control style" practiced by male leaders. Women oftentimes indirectly communicate their expectations of a given task and allow more space in accomplishing a goal. It sometimes helps the team members use their skills and expertise to complete the task, however, at other times it can be a drawback if the assigned task requires a leader to have direct communication with the members.

SELF-BRANDING

Unlike their male counterparts, women leaders often appear to be modest or silent about their accomplishments. They are seldom good at branding themselves. However, women leaders must learn how to brand themselves by sharing their achievements and skills with others. Unless people know or notice what they are capable of, they cannot recognize the leadership qualities of a woman leader. Women have often been branded with possessing "soft skills" which were viewed by men as weak with hints of complacency. However, recent research by McKinsey, Harvard and other notable research organizations have repeatedly proven that soft skills build loyalty, retention, and productivity, all of which enhance the bottom line. Despite these revelations, according to McKinsey (2021) only one in five leaders are a woman, and one in twenty-five are a woman of color.

WOMEN IN LEADERSHIP IMPORTANCE

Any institution, whether it is society or organization, in the present century cannot function effectively without women's equal participation in leadership activities. Women create a perspective that brings competition and collaboration to organizations and teams. According to the United Nations, there are currently twenty-five countries where women outnumber men. (24/7 Wall Street, Byrnes, Hristina, July 11. 2019)

In today's world, organizations that are led by inclusive leadership teams make effective decisions that deliver a better result. In the twenty-first century, the essential qualities required to lead include the ability to collaborate, connect, empathize and communicate. All these qualities are feminine in nature and can help build a more sustainable future.

Many statistics show that companies led by women have better financial results. Leadership by women is vital to increase the pace of societal transformation at home and in the workplace. Women leaders are likely to provide an integrated view of work and family, resulting in an engaged and promising personal and professional future. According to Fast Company, one area that organizations collectively spend billions on is engagement. Women leaders tend to drive higher engagement resulting in $1.43 million in savings for every 1,000 employees (Carter, 2022).

Gender parity in leadership is important because true progress cannot happen without a diversity of perspectives in leadership roles.

REPRESENTATION OF WOMEN IN DIFFERENT SECTORS

Representation of women in different sectors refers to the percentage of women employees working in various sectors. In the past, women were grossly underrepresented in politics, businesses, education, manufacturing, science, and technology, etc. However, this situation is slowly changing.

In the US, women are 50.8 percent of the total population. They earn almost 60 percent of undergraduate degrees and 60 percent of all master's degrees. They do fairly well in law, medical degrees, business administration, and management. Women account for 47 percent of the US labor force and 49 percent of the college-educated workforce.

Women in the US account for 52 percent of the professional-level and middle-management jobs. However, they lag substantially behind men when it comes to their representation in leadership positions. While 45 percent of the overall S&P (Standard and Poor's) and 37 percent of first or middle-level officials and managers in those companies, they make up only 25 percent of executive and senior-level official managers.

For women of color the statistics are much bleaker. With only 7 percent at the VP level and 4 percent at the C-suite level, proving a gross underrepresentation (McKinsey, 2021).

Women make up only 12 percent of governors and only 17 percent of the mayors of the 100 largest American cities. America trends behind our UK counterparts who have 30.8 percent of local councillors are women.

The above-mentioned facts and figures, though indicating a rise in women's representation in different sectors, show that women's representation in decision-making positions is far from being satisfactory. Much remains to be done to increase the number of women in strategic and decision-making positions.

Women are constantly evolving and reaching new milestones across a wide spectrum of human activities in modern times. The world has witnessed the advent of women leaders such as Hillary Rodham Clinton, Kamala Harris, Indra Nooyi, Oprah Winfrey, Theresa May, Christine Lagarde, to name a few.

Ursula Burns, previous CEO of Xerox company, shared her perspective as to why there aren't more women in leadership roles. She states the track to CEO positions for women of color isn't there because they are often shuffled into support roles: human resources, communications, public relations and community-based roles (Fortune, 2017). Women and women of color should seek out operational roles because they are more likely to lead to CEO positions. You have to be in a position that is close to the product and the money.

However, there is a need for further commraderie, mentorship, networking and knowledge sharing amongst the women that have made it, but once again women are asked to do more than their male counterparts at a time when women are grossly over committed.

Meanwhile, men will have to grasp that it is detrimental to their business and personal finances to continue leading organizations that are a monolith and not representative of our ever-changing globally diverse society.

I am also passionate about establishing corporate and entrepreneurial mentorship and sponsorship programs for women. These types of programs equip women with the critical information they need to manage successful careers and businesses.

THE REINVENTION REVOLUTION

AN EXECUTIVE WOMAN OF COMMAND

There's a distinct framework to becoming an executive woman of command. At the base of the pyramid is vision. The second rung of consist of goals. And the third rung, is Strategy with the final rung highlighting Outcomes. So, when you think of the framework for an Executive Woman of Command, it is thinking about what your intention is, what is it that you want to do? Who do you want to serve? What do you want your purpose to be? And then you have to focus on getting there.

Therefore, one might ask, what does it take to become an Executive Woman of Command? In addition to really understanding your intention, your focus, and your outlook, there's a series of initiatives that really make you a woman of command. I say start with the seven Rs, which is easy to remember and easier to apply to not only your professional life but also your personal life. One of the things that I really like to do is map them out, for women in general, but particularly executive women, or any woman that's the executive of her life. This might not mean that you work for a corporation or that you're becoming an entrepreneur, you can be the executive of your household, but what this is really about is to provide a framework that's really palatable and that you can execute and implement in a timely fashion without a lot of reading and researching on your own.

For me, I have nearly two decades of work experience, and my various work experience has gone from being an hourly employee, to an executive, to an entrepreneur. I have scaled all of the different facets of work life and personal life. I've been a union employee as well as a non-union employee, therefore I understand a lot of the nuances of being a professional in the workplace. And I think there's something to be said about who you seek advice from in your life. You really need to ensure that the information that you're getting is sound, that it's well researched, and that it's proven to provide value. So now let's talk about what those seven Rs are. We're going to dive deeper into each one of these as we go through the remainder of this book.

One is reinvention, and you might say reinvention means completely changing who you are. It doesn't, and we're going to talk more about what it really means, what it means to say yes, and the implications of saying no as you foster continuous improvement, to be cutting edge and relevant. We're going to talk about resilience. There's nothing in life that goes without bumps in the road. There's nothing that we involve ourselves in on a daily basis where we don't have to show resilience and fortitude in order to get through it. We're going to talk about that more in detail in terms of what that means and how individuals have proven to be resilient. And what does it take?

We're going to talk about restoration. What is restortion in the context of life and career? What does that mean when you are focused on achieving your goals, you have these intentions, you have focus, you have your outlook, now, how can you make sure you're restoring and replenishing what you need to do in order to move forward to your next step? How are you taking care of your mental health, your physical health, in order to get to the next step? And then we're going to talk about reliability, and what does that mean? Sometimes when you say yes to more than you can actually achieve on your plate, you get to the point of maybe not being reliable because you're not delivering. So what does it mean to be able to say yes, yet be reliable and deliver?

And then we're going to talk about being reflective. After you achieve all your goals and you're thinking about what you want to do next , what you've achieved, and now you're thinking about all of the things that you've gone through in life. How do you really sit and reflect upon what you've been through, where you are, and where you want to go next? What should those steps look like, and what should you be reflecting on in your life on a daily basis? And then we want to talk about reimagining. How do you then reimagine where you want to be, what your opportunities are, what you're capable of, what your purpose is? Next is resistance. These are all about being able to shoo away what isn't part of your intention, what isn't part of your focus, what isn't part of your outlook to keep you laser-focused on your outcome.

So how do you resist not only assignments or the next step in your career, or any myriad of what we think of as career issues, but how do you also resist negativity in your life, people that are in your circle that aren't in your corner? And that's extremely important in navigating your success. You can have people in your circle that are not in your corner. So we're going to talk about those seven Rs of success, reinvention, resilience, restoration, reliability, reflectiveness, reimagining, and resistance. Because, if you execute these seven Rs, you will gain life lessons on how to do that, and learn how to move from one step, to another. And most often, what I love to talk about is how these are transformative throughout your day, throughout your career, throughout your lifeline.

It's not like you have to follow one-through-seven in progressive order, "I'm going to focus on reinvention and then resilience and then being restorative, etc." No, any one of these can be part of your success soup on any given day. But being aware of them and also being interpersonally aware is going to help elevate you to the next level, and that's what we're really talking about here. And like I said, I'm going to give you examples of where I have helped others execute each one of these steps while providing stories and statistics on using the seven R's for sustainability and success.

Resiliency and Reinvention have been how I've survived in business and throughout my life. What I learned early in life, is that nothing stays the same. You must be adaptable, nimble, and knowledgeable. I experienced tragic losses in my life at a young age and because of that, I don't stay in any situation that steals my joy. I will not allow that to happen. It doesn't matter if it's with an employer, leader, friend, or in a relationship, life is too short for any form of extended misery or one-sided sacrifice. I want women to understand the art of reinvention and realignment, to take what they already know and package it differently. In your very first position, you will have acquired skills and knowledge that can prepare you for your next role in a completely different industry. You must have the confidence to value those skills and acknowledge you don't necessarily require a complete overhaul every time you want to pursue a new opportunity .

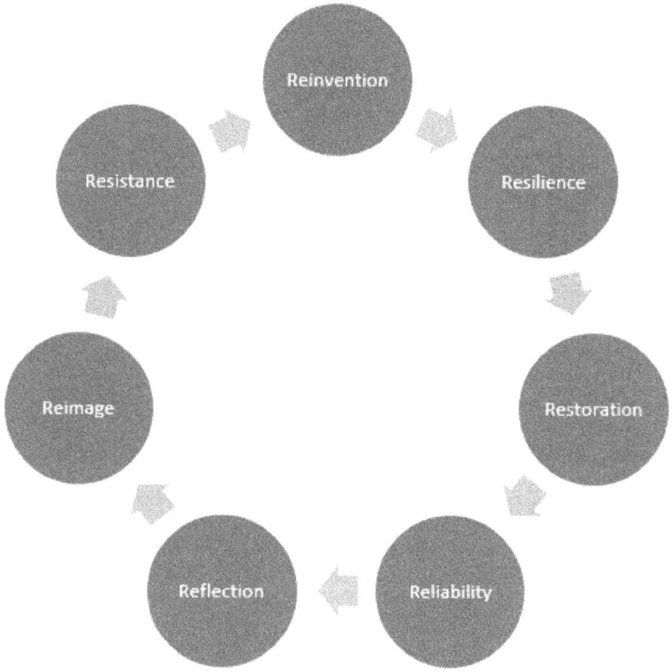

RE-INVENTION

Let's take a moment to think about what reinvention is. What do you visualize? What comes to mind when you think of reinvention? Generally, one thinks of new, different, innovative, relevant. According to Merriam-Webster, the definition of reinvent is to make as if for the first time something already invented. So when you think about self-reinvention, it really is to change the way that you behave or change your career, your profession, or the things that you do, so that people think of you as a different kind of person but also see you from a different vantage point. You often hear the term, "she has reinvented herself several times over". We often attribute this to individuals that are celebrities that are able to scale different types of roles, or being able to go from an actor/actress to an entrepreneur, a business owner, or a real estate developer or investor—that's reinvention. But wait? We are all capable of reinvention, not only celebrities.

When you're deviating from your core, you're deviating from what people typically think of you as. More often than not, it will come as a surprise to individuals because they may not have perceived you in that way, or they may not have ever considered that you could behave in a certain way or that you could transform yourself into something different, unexpected, fresh—and do it well. So when we think about what reinvention is, we've all reinvented ourselves. Our minds natually align change with reinvention. So, how do you build a "reinvention mindset"? At some point in our lives, the majority of individuals become the definition of whatever it is that they do most often. So for example, if you say, I am an accountant, then you will always see yourself as an accountant. And so if someone came to you and said, "Hey, how about you being an author? Or how about being an organization development specialist?" You might say, "No, I'm an accountant." And so when you have a reinvention state of mind, you have the ability to go from point A to point Z. This concept can be very surprising for individuals.

Let me give you a story of reinvention. Let's consider a couple of folks that we see and talk about all the time, a category of people referred to as celebrities.

Beyonce, a singer-song writer, actress, designer, business woman, producer, director and philanthoprist has been named the World's Greatest Living entertainer by Rolling Stone. This is quite an honor for a magazine established in 1967 and for a woman who began performing at eight years old when most of us were just trying to keep up with our classwork and friends.

Although, she has sold over 330 million records worldwide including 60 million from her time as a lead singer in Destiny's Child gifts others with her time, social clout and financial backing, donating millions to various philanthropic causes throughout her career. She often donates without public acknowledgment.

As you can imagine at 8 years old, she didn't know this would be her life and outcome. But the decisions that she made took her from good to great.

Starting out in local talent shows she was able to land a deal with Columbia records in 1997. But when offered the opportunity to act she didn't cower but ensured it was the right move in her career at the right time. It was a great opportunity for her initially playing the role of Carmen in *Carmen: A Hip Hopera* and her groundbreaking role with Mike Myers in the Austin Powers spy parody *Goldmember.*

Six years later she made another bold career move becoming a solo artist and releasing her *Dangerously in Love* album in 2003.

Relentlessly, managing her career, image, motherhood and being a wife she moved on to being the headliner at the SuperBowl, Coachella, providing the voice of the character Nala and performing songs in the movie *The Lion King,* designing a clothing line and beauty brand. She later expanded her creative prowless by writing, directing and producing many of her projects.

However, as with any of us in life she has not gone without some criticism which included her decision to perform for a Libyan leader, not singing completely live at President Obama's second inauguration and the latest using an ableist slur in one of her recordings. This is evidence that even the biggest pop star in the world, despite her accolades and successes have not gone without scrutiny. If you're going to be great and make an impact you will constantly have others judging you but it's how you decide to manage criticism that will elevate or sink you. When it matters, Beyonce will respond graciously and when it doesn't, she quietly handles the situation.

What's important to remember is no one is perfect. We all will make mistakes, that is a guarantee as living human beings. However, don't allow fear to stifle and smother your dreams. When we look at people in the public eye it's easy to focus on the glory and not the story. Reinvention is knowing that at some point things will not go as planned but having the wherewithal to persevere, even during challenging times. When you're in pursuit of your dreams know that there will be bumps in the road but how you decide to face and manage those obstacles will set the course for your continued success.

And I'll give you another great example of reinvention. Astrophysicist, Neil deGrasse Tyson, who specialises in a field which by all points and purposes is not a particulalry sexy field, unless you are interested in astronomy and astrophysics. It's not something you generally want to know about. It's remarkable how Neil deGrasse Tyson has made astrophysics a part of your everyday household, in ways where others have never managed to break through in the same way that he has. So let me talk you through his career and some of the things that he did because I want to provide you with great relevant examples of how you can take whatever it is you're doing now, and continue to excel and reinvent yourself.

Neil deGrasse Tyson became an astrophysicist in 1991, and by 1997 had created the department of astrophysics as part of the American Museum of Natural History. From there, he became an author and that's not unusual. So I would say that's not a huge reinvention to go from being an astrophysicist to an author, right? But it was the type of books he authored, for example: *Astrophysics for Dummies*. Well, if he can transform this to a venacular that is understandable by the majority of the population, then that is a huge accomplishment. It made regular, non-scientific people want to know more about astrophysics. *Astrophysics for Dummie*s became a wildly successful book and even I have it on my shelf. He gave people a basic understanding of what astrophysics entailed. Based on the success of his book and his several media appearances, in 2015 he was given the opportunity to host his own talk show called *StarTalk* on the National Geographic Channel. And from there, he continued to build his personality in an outward-spiral fashion. Meaning he went from podcasts to national geographic, to appearing on major networks like CBS news networks, MSNBC, CNN, HBO, to then appearing on top-rated TV shows such as *The Big Bang Theory* and *Real Time with Bill Maher,* to finally creating his own video game. All very different tracks. So being able to create various verticals for yourself is all part of the reinvention. I'm stressing it so much because many of us don't look at it this way. Many individuals become afraid of what might transpire if your reinvention doesn't turn out the way that you planned or the way that you think that it should. So people become paralyzed by fear and further paralyzed by individuals who might question their intentions. That questioning manifests into inaction because you no longer believe in yourself.

Others questioning your intentions in a way that is not constructive, can stimulate imposter syndrome. Not believing in yourself can also be imposter syndrome. Imposter syndrome can impact people in different ways. For example, if you can't imagine your dreams coming to fruition because you are not good enough or deserving or you make excuses. You say to yourself, things came easy for someone else because they had star power, they came from money, they are smarter than me, they know people in power. No! You might say, well, now those folks are stars or even they're huge, big stars and people: that's what they do. And they have the opportunity to do that. And they have coaches that help them along the way to be excellent.

Honestly, when others have access it can be an advantage, however the point of these stories is to demonstrate that some individuals that are successful came from humble beginnings. So, I'll use myself as an example of reinvention.

The everyday person who's not had a "Hollywood lifestyle" at all. I started out as a library assistant, not even earning a salary. Then I became a receptionist, a cashier, a telemarketer (literally selling coupons on the phone), I sold encyclopedias, I became an office manager, a flight attendant, a waitress, a temporary worker, but then continued on reinventing myself through all of those different career paths. Many of my peers that became flight attendants stayed in the field or stayed because they lacked the ability to parlay their skills into other fields outside of the aviation industry. It was a great career, decent pay, along with a lot of perks and accolades at the time, so they remained and became comfortable despite having the desire to do more in their careers. In addition, if you stayed in the industry for ten years, you received lifetime benefits. And it's actually a great job: you get to travel the world, meet all these cool people. You can make a decent living, great insurance, wonderful perks. Most people stay right there. So you might say, what was it about you that made you want to leave? And I'll say this. I always look for the next thing because that's how you stay cutting edge. That's how, when the economy is horrible, you either squeak by or do wonderfully because you have more hats in your basket than other folks to draw upon. So if you only have one hat in your basket, and someone takes that one hat from your basket, your basket is now empty, right? But if you have three or four hats in your basket and someone takes one, you still have a choice of three others. And that's no different than life. That's no different than how we think of ourselves. Every day we have to continually look to develop ourselves for the future. So that if the one thing we're doing today is no longer relevant, we are not only equipped to reinvent ourselves but that we can do it with confidence and ease because that's what's necessary. So I went on to become a technical recruiter. I knew nothing about it: coding, programming, technology, etc. I had to learn. I reinvented myself. I excelled and continued to grow and developed my career in human resources, employee relations, learning and development, diversity, equity and inclusion, and organization design.

Once I plateaued as a corporate executive, I thought, what can I do next? So people began reaching out to me to help their organizations, even though I was fully employed. I said to myself, let's do this, let's help the couple organizations and before long I was an entrepreneur. I had my own business in my mid-twenties, not once, but three times inventing and reinventing various businesses throughout my career. Each time I've developed a different type of vertical for my business. The first time I was doing diversity training and diversity recruitment. And then I transitioned that business to resume writing and career coaching. And then I transitioned to organization development; designing diversity, equity, and inclusion solutions, and now leadership development along with a business solely focused on women's personal and professional development.

From these experiences, I saw there was a need in the diversity space for us to close the gap on the polarization that was happening in the country. People on the left or the right. No one's in the middle. No one is talking to one another, there are folks on social media screaming and yelling at each other, arguing with individuals that they went to high school with that they've known for twenty-plus years or simply just writing them off because they have an opposing political view. Or they said something from a social standpoint that they didn't agree with. No one is talking. No one is trying to understand the other person's point of view. And so I decided I needed to help remedy this. So I wrote a diversity journal, called, *Who Are We? Broadening Your Perspectives*. It's designed to take people through a journey of understanding another person's journey, life and point of view.

I received requests from several professionals asking me to speak at their organizations. Speaking at various organizations is an enormous responsibility but it brought me so much joy. However, responsibility and venturing into new waters is never without some level of fear. But once again, reinvention is the catalyst. When I was a library assistant, when I was a flight attendant, I never, ever dreamed I would be a keynote speaker with a platform earning compensation for my thoughts, my ideas, my perspectives, my position, my knowledge. But I did. And YOU can too.

As famously stated by Theodore Roosevelt: "Nothing worth having comes easy." Building the life you want is about having that tenacity, having belief in yourself, and going after it. You're not going to be successful in everything you do. People aren't necessarily successful in every job they take, but they'll continue to take jobs in the same functional area, time and time again because that's what people do. But every time you start a new job, that's also a mini reinvention. It's a new culture. There are new people, there are new systems. There are new expectations. There are new leaders that you're reporting to. It's not an easy task going from one organization to another. It's a mini reinvention, 100% of the time, but most people don't view it that way. They don't view it in the same way as they would view going from a functional area of expertise to doing something you haven't done before. But just because you're leaving company A to go to company B and become a financial analyst, or an accountant, or a human resources manager, doesn't mean that it doesn't come without risk as well. So we just sometimes have to retrain our brains on how we think and look at things through a different lens and a different perspective.

I have broken glass ceilings throughout my professional and

academic career many times throughout my life, including;

- as a teenager asking that Black History be taught in my school district,
- being the only Black Editor-in-Chief of my High School newspaper,
- being the first Black female to win two best paper awards at my University,
- being the first Human Resources professional to win the Professional Recognition for Integrity, Dedication and Excellence at my previous employer with the least amount of tenure with the organization,
- being the only Black woman awarded the Visionary award in 2019 at my alma mater
- being the only two-time Notable Business winner in Illinois through my consulting firm.

What does reinvention do? How does it help you? Reinvention helps you remain relevant. It shows that you're not only relevant, but you're resilient. It also demonstrates you're a risk-taker because you are willing embark upon new endeavors. A characteristic of being an Executive Woman of Command is saying, "I'm willing to take that risk." Now we want to make sure we measure our risk. We don't want to recklessly take on various endeavors where we haven't researched well and can't make a viable connection, or we get that feeling in the pit of our stomachs not because of nervousness or butterflies, but because we know it's not the right thing. We're not talking about that. We're talking about being able to wrap your arms around new things, new endeavors that will help elevate you and help get you to where you want to be, and help add another hat to your basket. We are taught from a traditional perspective to go to school, focus on one area, do well in that area, excel in that area, retire and live a happy, nice pension-filled life.

Unfortunately, we have discovered that's not how it is anymore, and it is not how it is going to be ever again in our capitalist-centric society. Let's just take a look at one organization that stomped on the dreams of their 20,000 employees.

Enron, the darling of Wall Street, was once the seventh largest organization in the United States, worth about $70 billion. However, the top executives in the company sold their stocks earning billions, leaving the company completely bankrupt with retirement funds and pension plans depleted in 2001. There were no dollars remaining for those 20,000 employees that went to work everyday thinking their retirement and lives were going to be comfortable. These employees, regardless of age, had to start over at a time when other corporations didn't want to hire Enron employees due to the scandal that was associated. When you are forced to reinvent yourself it doesn't feel rewarding, instead it leaves a feeling of stress, despondence, anxiety, guilt and anger.

We're going to have to become very familiar with the gig economy. We're going to have to be familiar with reinventing ourselves and doing different things with different types of individuals in different types of organizations, in different types of industries. Because when one hat is taken, we want to be able to have other hats in our basket and the problem now, and the suffering, the pure suffering that so many people have right now, is that they have that one hat. They have bedazzled that hat, adding diamonds, bells and whistles, tinsel, feathers. That hat is a hat that should be in a museum. But when someone takes the hat, all the extras that you've added to that one hat are gone, you no longer have the diamonds, the tinsel. The fancy hat with all of its features is gone.

But when you have other hats in that basket, even if they took your best hat, you have others to draw upon. How does that relate, professionally? Well, for example, imagine you went to school for a functional area, or you are a traditional vocational expert; maybe you didn't need to go to school; maybe you have a certification; maybe you don't have a certification. You've just done something enough that you're an expert in it. I mean, you have put everything into that one area of expertise. You gave it all you had. Now imagine that area of expertise is no longer valued or no longer needed at a particular time. All of a sudden you have nothing to draw upon because you weren't making other hats along the way. You weren't putting other hats in your basket. You weren't replenishing your basket, your basket emptied because you focused all of your energy on glorifying your one and only hat.

And so when there is an economic downturn, if you have a lot of hats in your basket, then you can navigate, right? So for instance, I have a really great friend that is a bartender. When the bar shut down, he was fine, because he is also a hairstylist. When that shut down, he had his real estate agent license. And as those industries started to come back, he was able to come back and put those hats on. But when those hats were taken away, he had other hats to draw upon. He wasn't just reliant on his first, favorite hat. Being a bartender, he made great money. He worked at one of the top places where money flowed freely, where it's easy to sit back on your laurels, but instead he said, "Okay, this is going wonderfully. I am making great money doing this, but what is my backup plan?" He took a portion of his earnings and reinvested, going to cosmetology school and obtaining a real estate license.

Conversly, another person left the airline industry to waitress. Each night, she was earning three times the salary that she earned as a flight attendant, but instead she continued to waitress, knowing not only her body was ailing but she was literally aging out of that particular business model and industry. Despite having warnings for a couple of years, she was ultimately terminated, and had no other viable skills to rely upon that didn't include her being on her feet continuously for long periods of time. She was financially ruined but had no inspiration or belief in herself. Instead she became very comfortable with not being able to support herself; playing on other's pity because she refused to take any accountability for her outcome.

So having other things to draw upon is critial in today's marketplace. It's important to think about what would you do if your current career was no longer an option? Just visualize this, close your eyes for a moment. Visualize if your job went away tomorrow and what you did was no longer in demand, what would you do next? And if you can't answer that question, it's time to start thinking about reinvention.

MORE ON REINVENTION

Michelle Obama

Michelle Obama rocketed into the American consciousness shortly after her husband's speech at the 2004 Democratic National Convention, where he galvanized voters and launched his national political career. In those early days, reporters grappled with how to describe the statuesque wife of Illinois state senator, Barack Obama. Some, besotted by her flawless fashion choices, likened her to Jacqueline Kennedy, while others, noting her deep intelligence, invoked Eleanor Roosevelt. But neither description seemed quite right. And from the outset, Michelle evaded classification as a political plus-one, destined instead to become a force in her own right.

She was, for starters, never just a senator's wife. The impressive 5-foot-11 Michelle was a Princeton- and Harvard-educated attorney in possession of sharp wit, formidable ambition—and arms that would make a gladiator blush. Some political spouses such as Hillary Clinton embraced the limelight, and others, such as Barbara Bush, opted for domesticity, Michelle Obama fit neither mold. She told anyone who would listen that she hated politics, and yet she seemed also to chafe at expectations that she play a deferential role. Although, it wasn't always easygoing.

During her husband's first presidential campaign, critics slammed Michelle for "over sharing" when she joked about his morning breath, and she regularly made headlines—both glowing and scathing—for her unguardedly expressive face. (In 2013, Buzzfeed compiled a list of Michelle's 38 greatest facial expressions, many of which reappear in GIFs and jokes online today.) In one particularly memorable gaffe, Michelle told a campaign rally, "For the first time in my adult lifetime, I am really proud of my country." The comment drew fury from Republicans and sparked a national conversation about the complex patriotism often required of black Americans.

But in emerging into the searing limelight, Michelle Obama also found her way, quietly becoming something of an idol for American women trying to make their way in a career-driven world. Michelle was not just a political wife and the mother of two beautiful girls. And she was not just an ambitious lawyer of her own. She was, unapologetically, both. In campaign speeches, and later, in countless addresses as First Lady, she celebrated her roles, inviting voters into the ups and downs of her family life, joking about her husband allowing the bread to go stale on the counter, and expertly articulating the complex challenges facing young Americans today.

Michelle, who was raised in modest means on Chicago's South Side, seemed to give credence to the possibilities that America offered—and to add urgency to efforts to equalize access to real opportunity. When she spoke about the Obama administration's efforts to help students repay massive debt, voters had reason to believe her. "You're looking at a young couple that's just a few years out of debt," Michelle told a crowd, referring to herself and her husband. "See, because, we went to those good schools, and we didn't have trust funds." She went on to jokingly say: "I'm still waiting for Barack's trust fund."

If she was once reticent about politics, Michelle embraced her role as First Lady, using her podium at the White House to become a fitness leader, an advocate for healthy eating, and a persistent example of grace and poise. If her predecessor Laura Bush had been known for her flawless etiquette, Michelle's charm was somewhat more earthy. Her language was often peppered with the jargon of pop culture and references to TV shows, and she spoke openly and bluntly about life's challenges. She had every right to be pretentious, but somehow, she was utterly without pretension. Even showcasing her dancing skills on the Jimmy Fallon late night talk show.

And she managed to do it all, as was said of Ginger Rogers, "backwards and in heels." As the country's first African American First Lady, Michelle carried the additional responsibility, fairly or not, of representing an often underrepresented community. In an essay on TheRoot.com, Kim McLarin described Michelle and Barack's relationship as validation for Black women. "He chose one of us, and I am thrilled," McLarin writes. "She loves, respects, and adores Barack, but she is the prize and she damn well knows it. He better know it, too." In 2008, *Ebony* magazine named the Obamas on its 10 Hottest Couples list, alongside Beyoncé and Jay-Z.

As her time in the White House drew to a close, and the venomous 2016 presidential campaign reached a crescendo, Michelle took on a new role—that of the fiery orator. In a memorable speech at the 2016 Democratic National Convention, it was Michelle Obama who, this time, gave a speech that galvanized the crowd. Touching on race, partisanship, patriotism, and feminism, her words united a divided arena and offered an upbeat version of how far America has come.

Those themes are also present in her 2018 autobiography, *Becoming,* which has sold more than 10 million copies (another million copies went to a charity for education). And while her book tour created a tsunami of interest and applause, Former First Lady Michelle Obama remained grounded, her legacy clear. She has emerged as one of the most loved American icons representing grit, grace, humility—and the importance of nutritional health and physical fitness for Americans and particularly African Americans.

Oprah Winfrey

Oprah Winfrey, the richest African American woman in the United States of the twenty-first century, was born in Kosciusko, Mississippi in 1958, on the 29th of January. She is best known as the most successful American television producer, host, and philanthropist and is among the most influential women in the world. She did not have a promising childhood and had to face a variety of hardships in her teenage life. After her parent's separation, she was sent to her grandparents, to live in extreme poverty. Some say that she wore dresses made of a potato sack. She reunited with her mother at the age of six who moved with her to Milwaukee, Wisconsin. Her mother spent all day working as a maid at households and had no time for little Winfrey. At the age of nine, as she says, she was raped by her cousin, her uncle, and a family friend. Having had enough, she ran away from her home at the age of thirteen and became a mother at fourteen. After her son died in infancy, she went back to live with her barber father in Tennessee. This was the first time, as she remembers, she took her studies seriously and managed to become an honors student. Her dedication soon paid off and she became the most popular student at East Nashville High School and won several awards in open speech competitions. At the age of seventeen, she won the Miss Black Tennessee beauty pagent. Later, she studied communication at Tennessee State University. A prize from winning the pagent crown was being offered an on-air job at WVOL, a radio station serving the African American community in Nashville (Pageant Planet, 2022).

At the age of nineteen, her life took a turn for the better when she got a job as a co-anchor for the local evening news. In 1984, she started to host *AM Chicago*, an early morning talk show, which soon became the most-watched show in America. Later, it was renamed as *The Oprah Winfrey Show*. The syndicated talk show became the most popular show in television history with over 30 million American viewers and spanning across 144 countries worldwide.

Besides being a TV host and producer, she is the co-founder of OWN (Oprah Winfrey Network) and the founder of *Oprah Magazine*. In 1998, she started a charity named "Oprah's Angel Network" for which she carries all administrative costs. Oprah's Angel Network donated $10 million after Hurricane Katrina and collected $11 million given by her viewers at her request. She is regarded as the 32nd most philanthropic person in the world. In 2005, *Businessweek* enlisted her name among the 50 most generous philanthropists for her contribution which was equivalent to $303 million. According to *Forbes,* 2022, her net worth is $2.5 billion.

At the 2002 Emmy Awards, she was the recipient of the first Bob Hope Humanitarian Award for her contribution to television and films.

What is significant to note from Oprah's bio is that she took several chances and risks beginning in her teenage years and at sixty-eight years old, shows no sign of slowing down. She has grown from grocery store worker >pageant winner>radio host>anchor>talk show host> actress>tv producer>movie producer>network owner>spokeperson>author>publisher and more.

In addition, to all of her prestigious accolades, according to Gallup's annual most admired poll, she is consistently ranked as one of the most admired women in the world.

The time is now to seize your dreams. Although there is a perception of women that can be extremely limiting, we have to look beyond that and focus on what makes us unique. That will always be your secret sauce and it's generally what others might say that will hold you back. Be memorable. Oprah had presence and was a memorable person. She never lost sight of who she was.

There are three distinct attributes that will always encourage people to remember me:

- My unique name
- My height
- My laugh and my ability to make people feel as if they are the only person in the room

Do you know your three most memorable attributes? If not, take time to reflect. It's also okay to ask those close to you their thoughts on your three attributes. However, you must own and feel proud showcasing these attributes.

Queen Latifah

Queen Latifah worked hard to get where she is today. Lance Owens, a police officer, and Rita Owens are Queen Latifah's parents. Her given name is Dana Elaine Owens. Her Muslim cousin called her "Latifah," meaning sensitivity and delicateness in Arabic. Later on, Dana added Queen to her name to embrace the power in her African culture. Born in New Jersey, she is known to be an actress, music producer, writer and, hip-hop artist. Queen Latifah is a multitalented woman who is determined when it comes to succeeding.

Many things could have stopped Latifah from succeeding. "Latifah's 24-year-old policeman brother, Lance Jr., died in a motorcycle crash aboard a bike Latifah had given him just two months earlier" ... "Latifah and her friend Sean Moon, 22, were carjacked while in her $75,000 BMW in New York City's Harlem neighborhood. Moon was shot in the abdomen - and barely escapes death" (Celebrity Central/ Top 25 Celebs /Queen Latifah Biography). Even though she's had some rough times, such as losing her brother, Dana keeps getting better when showcasing her many talents. Everyone has a special talent that they do best. Queen Latifah is best known for her social politics as well as for her gift of rhyme. She has won many awards. The Queen was the first hip-hop artist to receive a star on the Hollywood Walk of Fame. Latifah is a woman of power from the heart. She didn't think about being famous and having money when starting her career. She did it because she enjoyed doing it. The money and being famous were just extras. Queen Latifah has become financially secure through her accomplishments.

Queen Latifah is one of the most multitalented women this world has to offer. In addition to music, movies, and television, Latifah also found time to author a book on self-esteem, entitled *Put on Your Crow*n (Dargis, Manohla). At the age of eight, she played in her first movie, *The Wizard of Oz*. She made her first album and added opera to one of her songs. Her lyrics are meaningful. She sings about strong women. After releasing her best-selling memoir and her fifth album, and making *PEOPL*E's Most Beautiful list, Latifah endorses Cover Girl cosmetics (Celebrity Central/ Top 25 Celebs /Queen Latifah Biography). Latifah doesn't just act, sing, produce tons of albums and write; her other talent is beauty because she has shown the world that beauty comes in different complexions and sizes. She is a respected woman by many people.

When it comes to succeeding, Queen Latifah is determined. Being eminently hardworking has brought her extremely far in life. She is now known to be full of talent. Life would be boring if her talent had not been expressed starting at such a young age. She had time, and it made her better. Queen Latifah is very inspirational. She shows the world that she is at the top. She makes her label noticeable. She becomes more of a "queen" every day. Queen Latifah isn't only a celebrity, she is also a neverending legend.

Kamala Harris

Harris, 56, is known for many firsts. She has been a county district attorney; the district attorney for San Francisco—the first woman. She has several firsts in her role as Vice President: the first woman, the first African-American woman, the first Indian-American, and the first Asian-American. When Democratic presidential candidate Joe

Biden picked Harris in August 2020 as his running mate, recognizing the crucial role Black voters could play in his determined bid to defeat Donald Trump, the then California Senator was the third woman to be selected as the Vice President on a major party ticket. Previously, Alaska Governor Sarah Palin in 2008 and New York Representative Geraldine Ferraro in 1984 were the other two.

Before becoming Biden's running mate, Harris had presidential dreams, which she abandoned due to lack of the financial resources to continue her campaign. She was of the only three Asian Americans in the Senate, she's the first Indian-American ever to serve in the chamber and she's one of only 11 blacks to serve as senator in their 232-year history (CNN, January 25, 2022).

During the Obama era, she was popularly called the "female Obama". A decade ago, journalist Gwen Ifill called Harris "the female Barack Obama" on the *Late Show With David Letterman*. Later, a small businessman from Willoughby Tony Pinto called her "a young, female version of the president".

She is considered to be close to Barack Obama, the first Black American President, who endorsed her in her various elections including that of the US Senate in 2016.

Harris was born to two immigrant parents: a Black father and an Indian mother. Her father, Donald Harris, was from Jamaica, and her mother, Shyamala Gopalan, immigrated to the US from Chennai in 1958. She, however, defines herself simply as "American".

After her parents divorced, Harris was raised primarily by her Hindu single mother. She says that her mother adopted Black culture and immersed her two daughters —Kamala and her younger sister Maya—in it. Harris grew up embracing her Indian culture but living a proudly African American life. She often joined her mother on visits to India.

Her maternal uncle Gopalan Balachandran, who is based in Delhi, described Harris as a "fighter" and expressed the hope her top-level position would give Indians in the US "greater access" in interacting with the US administration.

"My mother understood very well that she was raising two Black daughters," she wrote in her autobiography *The Truths We Hold*. "She knew that her adopted homeland would see Maya and me as Black girls and she was determined to make sure we would grow into confident, proud Black women."

Harris was born in Oakland and grew up in Berkeley. She spent her high school years living in French-speaking Canada—her mother was teaching at McGill University in Montreal.

Her mother told her growing up, "Don't sit around and complain about things, do something," which is what drives Kamala every single day, according to the Biden-Harris joint campaign website. "The first Black and Indian-American woman to represent California in the United States Senate, Kamala Harris grew up believing in the promise of America and fighting to make sure that promise is fulfilled for all Americans," it says.

She attended college in the US, spending four years at Howard University, which she has described as among the most formative experiences of her life. After Howard, she went on to earn her law degree at the University of California, Hastings and began her career in the Alameda County District Attorney's Office. She became the top prosecutor for San Francisco in 2003, before being elected the first woman and the first Black person to serve as California's attorney general in 2010, the top lawyer in America's most populous state.

In her nearly two terms in office as attorney general, Harris gained a reputation as one of the rising stars of the Democratic Party. She was elected as California's junior US senator in 2017.

"Kamala has spent her life fighting injustice. It's a passion that was first inspired by her mother, Shyamala, an Indian-American immigrant, activist, and breast cancer researcher," says her website. After all, her parents met at a Civil Rights event.

Harris has been married to Douglas Emhoff, a lawyer, for the past six years. She is the stepmother of two children, Ella and Cole who are her "endless source of love and pure joy". Biden stated that he would be honored to be serving with Harris, who will "make history as the first woman, first Black woman, first woman of South Asian descent, and first daughter of immigrants ever elected to national office in this country".

What I like about Kamala's story is that she had her own aspirations to become President. However, when that didn't work out, she had to check her ego and understand the impact she could have as Vice-President. It's not an easy decision to walk away from your personal aspirations to help someone else achieve theirs, taking the second-place position. She saw the opportunity of being a partner to accomplish a common goal, not just for herself but, for the benefit of the country.

I've been in the second-place position and it's not always easy to accept when you feel you deserve to be first. However, it's humbling to realize that there may be a learning opportunity in the second-place position. Never stop being a steward of learning and enriching yourself. You can take away something positive or constructive from almost any situation you encounter.

CARRIER STATISTICS, FACT AND MAJOR KEYS

STATISTICS SUGGEST YOU WILL CHANGE CAREERS MORE FREQUENTLY

The average person will change careers five to seven times during their working life according to career change statistics. With an ever-increasing number of career choices, 30 percent of the workforce will now change careers or jobs every twelve months.

By the age of forty-two, you may already have had about ten jobs. [The Department of Labor (D.O.L)]

AM I MAKING A CAREER CHANGE OR A JOB CHANGE?

One of the problems when assessing career change statistics is to differentiate between making a job change and making a career change. For example, if a schoolteacher secures a new job as a corporate sales trainer, has she changed careers or just changed jobs? You could argue that she has changed careers from education to sales. Or you could argue that she has changed jobs from schoolteacher to adult teacher.

What about someone who transitions from a sales representative to a marketing manager? You could argue that they have not changed careers because they are still in the sales field. But marketing experts would say that sales and marketing are two completely different fields and that this transition does constitute a career change.

WHAT DO THESE CAREER CHANGE STATISTICS TELL US?

If you are going to change careers, you should plan for it! Plan financially, plan by proactively setting up networks and understand how to market yourself, and plan to potentially engage in some career change training.

Employers expect, or at least accept, that workers will be changing jobs a lot more often these days—about every three years with the younger generation at an even faster rate. According to Axios Gen Z'ers are changing jobs at 134% higher than they were in 2019, with many stating they are the responsible for driving their own careers.

If you are changing jobs less than every three years, you are in the minority. You may need to have an explanation when you prepare for your next job interview about why you have changed jobs so frequently.

What causes workers to want to change careers every three years?

- Do we simply get bored or is it the result of having more and different career choices?
- Do we become more aware of our gifts and abilities as we progress in our careers?
- Is three years about how long it takes for people to run into

work culture problems or personal conflicts in their working environment?

WHAT ARE THE MOST COMMON REASONS FOR CAREER CHANGE?

Career change statistics from the D.O.L don't tell us much about why people change jobs. But here are some likely reasons based on other sources:

- Lack of career development and training.
- Frustration and disillusionment – not using my natural abilities in my current job.
- Not happy with management.
- Redundancy or business closure.
- Working in a diminishing industry.
- Realignment of personal or spiritual values (i.e.) a midlife re-evaluation.
- Dislike of the organizational culture.
- Want more money!

THE PROS AND CONS OF MAKING A CAREER SWITCH

So career change statistics suggest we will change jobs more often but is this a good thing?

Some benefits of a frequent career change are:

- Less likely to get bored.
- You will get to experience a greater variety of job types and organizational cultures.
- You will meet more people (which is ideal for networking for your next job).

Some negative results of this could be:

- Having different career choices available means that you might be tempted to change careers too frequently.
- Prospective employers may think "hey this person will be gone in twelve months," thereby making them reluctant to employ you.
- You may also miss out on the opportunity to climb the ladder within an organization simply because you aren't there long enough.
- Some people may also make some unreasonable judgments on your stability and effectiveness as an employee.

A GOOD REASON TO CHANGE JOBS

Career change information tells us that one of the most common reasons people leave a job is due to being dissatisfied and unfulfilled with the work they do.

According to Gallup, globally 80 percent of people are not engaged in their current job and the main reason for this is a mismatch of not doing what they do best everyday and feeling irrelevant; not recognizing how their jobs make a difference at the company or in the world (Gallup, 2022).

So we should always attempt to move closer to a job that uses our natural gifts, abilities and aligns with our values. This is the only way we can experience true fulfillment in our careers.

Assessments will highlight your stengths and opportunities so that you can not only discover what you naturally like to do but also determine where you thrive. Remember, everyone is great at something. Although, it is an investment of time, you will find the information invaluable to your ongoing development.

RISK AND PROSPECT THEORY

RISK

Relocating for a new opportunity is inherently risky. I've relocated several times for new career opportunities and in most cases, they were truly exciting, but in a few, there was a mismatch. In other situations, I was offered opportunities that I didn't accept because I wouldn't have enjoyed living in that particular city and state. It's important that the opportunity is worth the move when you are leaving behind your entire ecosystem and home. If you can't list three reasons why a relocation opportunity will enrich your life, you shouldn't move forward.

Choosing to go back to school for educational endeavors, as a working adult, is also a big risk. There are financial and time commitments involved. So many transitions can happen in your life in the two to five years it takes to pursue a degree or an advanced degree. One way I have rationalized any educational endeavor, is that time doesn't stop. Those years spent studying will inevitably pass and at the end of that time, I will have conquered the goal and my fear. Each time,

I was able to successfully reach my goal despite experiencing severe adversities and change.

Another of my inherent risks, is my knack for transitioning through many different employers and positions. I don't sit still for long in any one place. I've spent time assessing this and I realize it's simply how I'm wired, along with not allowing myself to be in situations that are not conducive to my well-being and mental health. Once again, my mental model is "life is short" and that means not putting up with anyone's BS!

According to Merriam-Webster, risk is defined the possibility of loss or injury. Risk inherently involves uncertainty about the effects/implications of activity with respect to something that humans value, often focusing on negative, undesirable consequences.

THINGS TO CONSIDER WHEN TAKING BIG RISKS IN LIFE

Accept and Embrace the Idea of Setbacks in Life

Regarding that paralyzing fear of failure, the first thing you need to do when you take a big life risk is accepting everything may not turn out exactly as you planned ... And that's okay! Have a backup plan for what you'll do if various obstacles arise. Also, know that as long as you draw an important lesson from each perceived failure then you'll still benefit from the experience.

According to Forbes, 90 percent of initial startups fail. Surprisingly, only 20 percent of the population set goals with 70 percent of them failing to achieve the goals they set for themselves.

I am sharing these statistics not to scare you but to motivate you. You must follow through on your goals and plans in order to experience success. You need to build the internal rigor of follow-thru, tenacity and even failure. Failure allows us to take the lessons learned allowing us to benefit from those teachings in the future.

Get the Facts

What are the most intimidating things about the big risk you're about to take? Once you've figured this out, do as much research as you can in order to better insulate yourself from negative outcomes. But it's important not to become a victim of analysis paralysis. That is where you become so engrossed in analysing every angle of a situation that it causes you not to act at all because you are focused on finding every nuanced factor before springing into action, and so you do nothing. This process also gives individuals, from their perspective, a definitive excuse for inaction because it gives the illusion of doing something, when in actuality you are hiding behind process because this absolves you from taking on an risk; from moving forward; to executing your plan.

For example, if you're trying to create a new business, look into the competing businesses already out there and ensure that you'll be offering something different, provide a different level of service or have a distinct way of differientating your business.

Take Risks for Yourself

If there's pressure from your family or wider social circle to go in a particular direction, you might want to take a big risk if it means you'll get their support and approval.

However, be aware so that you can resist this urge. It can feel euphoric to have the support of those closest to you but that doesn't ensure it's the right thing to do or not to do. You must be resolute in your direction and goals. Significant risks should only be undertaken if they're in your best interests and align with your dreams for the future. You're less likely to manifest a positive outcome if you aren't truly vibrationally aligned with your "goal". Plus, ask yourself whether the people who are applying pressure would come to your aid if you got into difficulty as a result of taking their advice.

Trust Your Intuition

All major Law of Attraction guides note the importance of trusting your intuition and developing this faculty so that you are able to pick up helpful cues and signposts from the universe. This is a particularly important piece of advice when it comes to risk-taking. If you're on the fence about something and you just have a feeling that it's right, take a deep breath and act.

Meanwhile, if there's a nagging sense that something isn't right, trust that feeling, continue to explore by writing out a pros and cons list. This simple task generally provides clarity to decision-making.

Make Sure Risks Are Worthwhile

Sometimes, you might prepare yourself to take big risks as part of your Law of Attraction journey and then be so committed to this bravery that you end up taking risks you don't really need to.

For example, it can be scary to put yourself out there to find a new position, but just because you've decided you are looking for a new job, doesn't mean that you accept every interview and opportunity presented to you.

In sum, even though you're committed to taking leaps of faith as part of your manifestation process, do take the time to weigh each individual risk and rewards on their own merits.

KNOW WHEN TO CHANGE COURSE

We don't always set the right Law of Attraction goal the first time. It's important that you avoid simply sticking to your first goal solely because you've invested time and effort.

Regularly consider the life-changing risks you're taking to see if you remain genuinely positive about the end product.

Know when it's time to quit, reevaluate, regroup and start on a new path.

Don't Be Afraid

Finally, it's only by being willing to take risks that you invite anything inspiring and exciting to happen in your life.

Try to keep that in mind whenever nerves threaten to overcome you. You could live a life without risk, but you'd never end up manifesting the things you desire most of all. In some ways, that's no life at all! But instead is a life that will be riddled with dismay, regret and unrealized success.

Alternatively, find out what is holding you back from taking these big risks. Depending on which research you subscribe to, Harvard, Newsweek or Forbes, along with how the research was conducted, men can be easily viewed as being larger risk-takers while women can be categorized as risk adverse. However, when you look outside of general business areas and to those that are more socially focused, women tend to be the larger risk takers. The United States has a history of rewarding people for exhibiting masculine qualities. However, this is shifting in a more balanced way.

10 COMMON TRAITS OF RISK-TAKERS

1. They are comfortable being uncomfortable

2. Like taking action
3. Know there is something better, more exciting, new
4. Know what they want
5. Curious
6. Can brush off failures
7. Decisive
8. Confident
9. Passionate
10. Trust their intuition

PROSPECT THEORY

WHAT IS PROSPECT THEORY?

Prospect theory assumes that losses and gains are valued differently, and thus individuals make decisions based on perceived gains instead of perceived losses. Also known as the "loss aversion theory", the general concept is that if two choices are put before an individual, both equal, with one presented in terms of potential gains and the other in terms of possible losses, the former option will be chosen (Pan, 2019).

KEY TAKEAWAYS

Prospect theory says that investors value gains and losses differently, placing more weight on perceived gains versus perceived losses.

An investor presented with a choice, both equal, will choose the one presented in terms of potential gains.

Prospect theory is also known as the loss-aversion theory.

The prospect theory is part of behavioral economics, suggesting investors choose perceived gains because losses cause a greater emotional impact.

The certainty effect says individuals prefer certain outcomes over probable ones, while the isolation effect says individuals cancel out similar information when making a decision.

HOW PROSPECT THEORY WORKS

Prospect theory belongs to the behavioral economic subgroup, describing how individuals make a choice between probabilistic alternatives where risk is involved and the probability of different outcomes is unknown. This theory was formulated in 1979 and further developed in 1992 by Amos Tversky and Daniel Kahneman, deeming it more psychologically accurate of how decisions are made when compared to the expected utility theory.

The underlying explanation for an individual's behavior, under prospect theory, is that because the choices are independent and singular, the probability of a gain or a loss is reasonably assumed as being 50/50 instead of the probability that is actually presented. Essentially, the probability of a gain is generally perceived as greater.

Tversky and Kahneman proposed that losses cause a greater emotional impact on an individual than does an equivalent amount of gain, so given choices presented two ways—with both offering the same result—an individual will pick the option offering perceived gains.

For example, assume that the end result of receiving $25. One option is being given $25 outright. The other option is being given $75 and then having to give back $50. The utility of the gaining $25 is exactly the same in both options. However, individuals are most likely to choose to receive only the $25 versus initially having $75. The perceived negativity in losing the other $50 is worse than having the $75 initially. A single gain is generally observed as more favorable than initially having more cash and then suffering a loss.

Although there is no difference in the actual gains or losses, prospect theory says investors will choose the product that offers the most perceived gains. This is also how people access gain and losses in decisions. The mere perception of loss will cause many to never seek the gain therefore becoming complacent and not fully realizing their potential. They can't fathom taking a risk and potentially losing.

SPECIAL CONSIDERATIONS

According to Tversky and Kahneman, the certainty effect is exhibited when people prefer certain outcomes and underweigh outcomes that are only probable. The certainty effect leads to individuals avoiding risk when there is a prospect of a sure gain. It also contributes to individuals seeking risk when one of their options is a sure loss.

The isolation effect occurs when people have presented two options with the same outcome, but different routes to the outcome. In this case, people are likely to cancel out similar information to lighten the cognitive load, and their conclusions will vary depending on how the options are framed.

EXAMPLE OF PROSPECT THEORY

Prospect Theory looks at risk from the perspective of gains. Thinking of gains can be difficult, as it is hard to envision what you don't see. For example, because there are only two African-American women CEOs in Fortune 500 companies in the United States, the risk becomes too great. It's impossible to see the gain in a situation where you have witnessed such limited success. So let's consider a women of color is being offered an opportunity for an executive level position in an organization where a woman of color has never been offered or been in an executive level role. Who wants to be the first? Who is willing to take the risk? To see the gain? Of course, we know that someone has to eventually eclipse the glass ceiling but consider the countless women of color that never saw the possibility because they never saw the gain in pursuing a path that seemingly leads to no where for 95 percent of women of color.

PROSPECT THEORY FAQS

What Does Prospect Theory Mean?

Prospect theory from an organizational development perspective says that team members value gains and losses differently. That is, if a team member is presented an opportunity based on potential gains, and another opportunity that has some abstractness and uncertainty based on potential losses, the team member will choose the opportunity where potential gains and less ambuguity are presented. Even more daunting, individuals might not put themselves on a more challenging career path because they feel they can't see what they want to become. They view non-representation as a loss.

Why is Prospect Theory Important?

It's useful to understand your biases, where losses tend to cause greater emotional impact than the equivalent gain. Prospect theory helps describe how decisions are made by team members and entrepreneurs.

What Are the Main Components of Prospect Theory?

Prospect theory is part of the behavioral economic subgroup. It describes how individuals make decisions between alternatives where risk is involved and the probability of different outcomes is unknown. There is a certainty effect exhibited in the prospect theory, where people seek certain outcomes, underweighting only probable outcomes.

Who Proposed Prospect Theory?

Prospect theory was first introduced in 1979 by Amos Tversky and Daniel Kahneman, who later developed the idea in 1992. The pair said that the prospect theory was better at accurately describing how decisions are made.

What Did Kahneman and Tversky Do?

Kahneman and Tversky proposed that losses have a greater emotional impact than a gain of the same amount. They said that, given choices presented two ways—with both offering the same result—an individual will pick the option offering perceived gains.

Bottom Line

Prospect theory says that individuals will accept an investment when the gains are presented, versus the losses. That is, individuals weigh potential gains more than potential losses.

RESILIENCE

If success, leadership, and fulfillment are why you went into business in the first place, then understanding how you respond to challenges, disappointments, and crises, is important. Resilience is the mark of all success stories, much as it is the mark of every good leader.

I allow myself a day to feel down. I feel anything beyond that is not generally helpful. I remember living in Seattle, WA and setting myself a goal of relocating back to Chicago, IL by the beginning of the following year. I was far from my natural support system, I wasn't working with a true leader and there were few career opportunities at the time because the country was in a dreadful recession. I had no idea what my next move would be, I just knew it wouldn't be there in Seattle, and that my place was back in my hometown. My resilience comes from constantly moving forward in some way. Looking ahead gives me energy, knowing something positive is on the horizon. Sometimes you just have to step out with faith and knowing in your heart and mind that everything will be okay. Embracing negativity nets negative outcomes. We realize what we socialize in our minds. It's extremely important for me to embrace positivity, even it means isolating for a while. You have to find your peace. There are also people, both professional and psychological, that can help us along in our journey. There will be times in your life, when your friends and family are not equipped to assist you with your concerns on a day-to-day basis. This is when you may need to seek out the help of a professional. These days, you can even use video-conferencing for these discussions, so they are not as cumbersome as in the past when the expectation was to physically go into an office.

Many people think resilience is just about bouncing back from a challenging time or getting over disappointment or experiencing a loss in your professional or personal life. It is that, certainly, but resilience is so, so much more.

For me, resilience is at the very heart of leadership. It matters because it's about how people adapt and then are able to move forward. Some of us can get over a hump or a challenge or a loss, or even around an obstacle, but if we never process what we did to surmount that challenge and overcome it, we're just setting ourselves up for more—and more disastrous—challenges in the future. Resilience is about overcoming adversity and "winning," but—perhaps more importantly—it's also about adapting to understand how we coped or didn't with certain challenges.

Author Jill Campbell says, "Resilience is really important. People whom I've seen succeed the most are the ones who get kicked in the teeth and get up quicker than anyone else. You know, they'll grieve, they'll feel sorry for themselves for ten minutes, and then they just rally. I think they're fearless, but it's not a reckless fearlessness. It's more a willingness to take risks, step out there, make mistakes, but not see that as the end of the world. So resilience is really important, particularly in moving up the ladder in your career. And sometimes you just have to accept a no, you know? That's the reality of how it works. You may have your heart set on something and it's just not going to happen and so you've got to know when to spend your time to get to 'yes' and when you just cut your losses [and move on]."

Triumphing over adversity is an admirable achievement, but if it doesn't become a transferable skill, or even a habit, it will never lead to true change, which after all is at the heart of resilience. The act of overcoming becomes a transformation. That is resilience. For me, one of the hallmarks of resilience is how people learn from challenges, adversity, failures, even lack of opportunity. For instance, watch what happens when resilient people don't get picked for something or if they miss out on a raise or an opportunity or a promotion or a leadership challenge. For instance:

- Do they give up and blame others? No.
- Do they storm out of their supervisor's office in the midst of a tantrum? No.
- Do they go around bad-mouthing whoever they perceive "robbed" them of their opportunity? No.
- Do they immediately go and vent on social media about the situation? No.

Sure, they may be hurt or disappointed or even jealous, but they don't let that stop the learning process. Instead, resilient people step back, assess the situation, do an "internal audit" and try to determine where they came up short. They ask:

- "Am I taking my job status too lightly?"
- "Am I getting too comfortable in my role?"
- "Have I been stuck in neutral too long and need to find another gear?"
- "Is my paperwork getting sloppy?"

- "Am I making my career intentions clear?"
- "Have I actively engaged in development opportunnities in the past year?"

We can all get into a rut in our work, but resilient people see disappointment, even failure, as an opportunity to shake the dust off, start anew, and reinvigorate their performance.

After her son Connor died in a boating accident when he was not wearing a life vest, Dana Gage founded the LV Project, which is dedicated to improving water safety and creating buoyancy in life. According to Dana, "You've got to be comfortable with discomfort. If you wait, you're never going to move forward with anything. You have to just keep walking forward. Don't be afraid of what might be across the bridge. What will happen will happen, so just accept that things are not always going to go well, and move forward anyway."

Throughout this book, I've asked you to do a few simple things to become confident to the core: Raise your hand more often. Get out there. Speak up. Stand out. And I realize that trying new things, particularly when you may not be used to them, often leads to disappointment. So maybe you've been doing those things, speaking up, standing out, asking more and it's just not going your way. You're not getting picked immediately; you may not be seeing direct results. Don't fret. Often, what you will learn when you are not selected is more important than what you may or may not learn when you are selected.

THE POWER OF RESILIENCE

Women are half the educated labor force and earn a large number of today's advanced degrees, yet outside academia women are still dismally behind in titles, promotions, and advancements.

The numbers are even more staggering for African American women, according to the National Center for Education Statistics, black women earned 66 percent of bachelor degrees and 71 percent of master's degrees from 2009-2010. However, we all know attainment of a degree cracks open the door but doesn't afford you the clearance to fully walk through (Davis, 2020).

Having the ability to be resilient—to bounce back, regroup, and lead and inspire others—is an enormously important attribute that could decide if a woman advances professionally or gets passed over for career opportunities.

Some women seem to be born resilient. For everyone else, there are learned skills that can increase our resiliency aptitude.

Having the ability to take whatever is dealt and still focus on staying on top of our game takes awareness, understanding, and action. Without this mindfulness, I've seen some incredibly bright folks become so entrenched in negative thinking that nothing can convince them there is hope or possibilities. Yet we can change the character of our lives by changing our beliefs.

THE POWERFUL CHOICE OF RESILIENCE

We get to choose how resilient we're going to be by how we respond to everything in our lives. It's all about being aware that things will continue to annoy or frustrate us and that not everyone will like us or our ideas. And that's OK. We are smart enough not to give away our power, and that means paying attention to how we're thinking and adjusting when necessary.

Here are some simple steps to boost your resiliency:

Understand the various facets of emotional intelligence. How and when you respond to certain events, comments and information overwhelmingly has an impact on our success and our reputation. When we cultivate the belief that internal fortitude, not circumstances, affects achievements, it enables us to bounce back no matter what.

After makinng the decision to take another corporate position, leaving Coleman & Associates behind, it didn't mean that the entrepreneur in me died. In fact, it was more present than ever. I had an advantage that my colleagues didn't in knowing what it takes to build and sustain a profitable business translating that knowledge into my current role. I was always able to understand viewpoints from both a customer perspective and business perspective. Having that experience built my resiliency versus taking away from it. We have to know what defines and differientates us personnally and professionally.

Think E R=O: An Event we have no control over, plus our Response, which we have every control over, has everything to do with the Outcome.

Get comfortable with being uncomfortable. To grow and become more resilient, we must get used to being uncomfortable. Once you settle on that, it's easier to use your voice and contribute. It becomes easier to have a differing opinion or perspective knowing that doing so will have some level of discomfort and investment.

Build your support network. The more allies we have personally and at work, the easier it is to have solutions when faced with challenges. Use emotional awareness, display empathy, communicate with compassion, and look at what you can do for others. The simple act of focusing on helping others enables us to be more effective in our own endeavors.

Show gratitude for all that you've accomplished. Today isn't where you will be tomorrow. When you are resilient and highly ambitious you focus so much on where you are going you don't take the time to reflect on where you have been and what's been accomplished along the way. I am guilty of this myself. Only when I was beginning to write this book did I take a hard look on the adversities I overcame, the various careers, the sheer passion it took to get to where I am today while knowing there is work to do.

Take time for you. Find some time to restore, reflect and rejoice regardless of your schedule or current sitation. It has been proven many times over, the importance self-care has on livlihood and lifespan. According to the Office on Women's Health, effectively managing stress has several health benefits: it strengthens your immune system, improves cognitive performance, lowers your heart rate, increases your energy, decreases weight gain and obseity and assists in managing anxiety and depression. This should be enough to realize how important self-care will be for you and your career.

Women often have the added burden of proving their own competence while facing the everyday challenges of a busy career.

Resilience is the skill that enables women of every age to cope, regroup, and model the attributes of leadership, wherever they are within an organization.

I believe resilience comes from within but also from dogged determination. Nothing fuels resilience as much as proving nay-sayers wrong. And that can include yourself as well. Resilience can come from both family and your environment. My Mother has always been the source of my common-sensical resilience. She told me I could be *anything* with focus, along with discipline, determination, and respect for others and myself. Many people go wrong with "you can be anything you want" - they leave off what my Mother always told me: "Yes, you can be anything you want, but it is contingent upon the effort you put into getting those results." I believe resilience is something you find within yourself when faced with unexpected adversity. There is an innate ability to keep going, believing in yourself, and never discounting the gravity of a win, big or small. Resilience also comes from feeding your philanthropic spirit. Helping others will often help us more than those we are assisting.

RESTORATION OF WOMEN IN LEADERSHIP

Women have increasingly moved toward greater gender equality at home and in the workplace. Yet, women are underrepresented in leadership roles, unequal to men in leadership roles across all industries. In examining differences between how men and women lead stereotypic gender role expectations, we can constrain leadership behaviors.

The perceived incongruity between women and leadership roles pose obstacles to leadership and result in double binds, more negative performance appraisals, and different standards compared to those applied to men.

It is increasingly clear that a gender-neutral view of leadership is insufficient, and that we need to consider the influence of cultural worldviews and socialization on shaping leadership style. There is much to suggest that feminist leadership styles are intentionally different—more collaborative and transformational compared to men.

This becomes more complex when we include dimensions of racial and ethnic diversity. We need to transform our views of leadership to promote more robust theories and diverse models of effective leadership. While current leadership theories favor transformational and collaborative leadership styles, organizational cultures often mirror social constructions of gender and ethnicity norms in society. Within the context of large organizations, there is often a tension between hierarchical and collaborative forms of leadership reflected in contradictory sets of practices. While women leaders may have an advantage in such contexts, they also face obstacles in needing to change organizational cultures that mirror social biases against women as leaders. In spite of the women's leadership style netting better overall results, women continue to be penalized and margainlized for these very leadeship competencies.

UNDERREPRESENTATION

Women have increasingly moved toward greater gender equality at home and in the workplace. Changes in gender roles and lifestyles have occurred with men now sharing more in household chores and childrearing. Social rules of etiquette and gender roles are now more flexible and equity within the marital relationship more common. Women are more able to navigate life in and outside the home easily and freely. Many women now work outside the home; in the U.S., they comprise 46 percwnt of the workforce. So much has changed; so much has not. One big shift in the United States is for men to request paternity leave to assist in the care of their children. Alexis Ohanian, Executive Chairman and co-founder of the social media site Reddit, make it socially okay for a man, even one in a senior level position to request paternity leave (Singh, 2022).

Women continue to be underrepresented in leadership roles

in corporations, institutions of higher education, and the political sector especially in light of the changing population demographics. In the U.S., women now make up 8.1 percent of Fortune 500 CEOs. (Hinchliffe, 2021). This was celebrated as if there isn't additional work to be done because having forty-one women CEOs is more than previously seen in CEO roles in American history. However, the picture become much bleaker for African American female CEOs. Currently, there are two, and in the history of the United States there have only been as many as four. The fact that I can recite these names without pause is disheartening.

Although there is work to be done in the field of academia, according to College and University Association for Human Resouces, the trending is a bit more positive, with 32 percent of colleges and universities having female Presidents, as opposed to the less than 8 percent in corporate America. However, the trend continues with minorities seeing a smaller share with only 17 percent being college presidents and 5 percent being women of color (Touchton, J. G. & Iomengram, D. 1995). In 2006, 86 percent were white and 23 percent were women with the majority of women presidents heading up small, private four-year universities or community colleges (June 2007). Women are still considered an anomaly compared to men when in high positions of leadership. Contradictory portrayals of women leaders pose obstacles to how they lead and often result in different standards than those applied to men. Women leaders are alternately portrayed as soft and ineffective, or domineering and manipulative. This picture is complicated by its interaction with racial and ethnic differences.

Is there a difference between men and women in how they lead?

The answer to this is complex; yes and no. Theories of leadership are typically neutral or absent in their attention to gender as if a leader is a leader, while studies on leadership typically ignore gender differences or mostly study white men. Popular wisdom and women's self-reports often identify distinct leadership styles and characteristics associated with gender while empirical studies on gender and leadership (e.g., Eagly & Johnson, 1990) often show that men and women leaders behave more alike than different when occupying the same positions. Why is it then that the strength of these perceptions persists? We often perceive traits associated with leaders that may not have much to do effective leadership; these characteristics are often embraced by leaders themselves. Terms like: he looks like a leader; he is presidential, charismatic, a visionary, are all terms used to define leaders. They often capture what followers want in their leaders—which, in turn, are influenced by social constructions of leadership which are associated with the social construction of gender roles and their resulting impact on leadership styles.

In a meta-analysis of gender and leadership style (Eagly & Johnson, 1990), gender differences did not emerge in organizational studies between interpersonal vs. task-oriented style. However, stereotypic gender differences did emerge in laboratory experiments and assessment studies, i.e., studies in which participants were not selected for holding a leadership position. Social perceptions and expectations influence the leadership styles of women leaning toward being more relationship-based when in situations of self-assessment or when appointed to leadership roles in laboratory studies. Men conformed more toward the social stereotypes of being more task-oriented, self-assertive, and motivated to master their environment, while women conformed more toward social stereotypes of being more interpersonal, selfless, and concerned with others. This is often distinguished as a person orientation over task orientation with women viewed as having an advantage (Bass & Avolio, 1994; McGregor, 1985).

There is strong evidence to support the tendency for women to adopt a more collaborative, cooperative, or democratic leadership style and for men to adopt a more directive, competitive, or autocratic style; this emerged in all types of studies. Even though selection criteria for leadership positions may even out the gender differences, women seem to be intentionally different and more collaborative based on differences in personality and social/interpersonal skills. The use of a collaborative process is increasingly central to views of effective leadership.

Is there a bias against women leaders?

People often associate qualities to leaders that are inherent in the personality of the leader. They may view leaders as inspiring followers to behave according to the purposes of the leader, including:

- a role model (i.e., setting an example),
- talent in having a specific skill for the organization,
- initiative and entrepreneurial drive,
- charisma (i.e., attractiveness to others and the ability to leverage this esteem to motivate others),
- inspirational (i.e., instill passion or cultivating an environment that brings out the best of individuals),
- commitment or visionary (i.e., clear sense of purpose or mission-driven).

However, it is unclear how dimensions of gender, race, and ethnicity confound these assessments of leadership and the conferring of leadership status.

Aversive sexism and racism (Eagly & Karau, 2002) suggest that perceived incongruity between female gender roles and leadership roles leads to prejudicial appraisals of women leaders. Women as leaders can be perceived as emotional versus being viewed as having value-added soft skills Eagly (1987) also found that women leaders were evaluated differently and less favorably than men even when performing the same leadership behaviors. Thus, social perceptions and expectations often result in more exacting standards for women and ethnic minorities than those applied to white men. These biases have also been identified by Dovidio and Gaertner (1996) in unintentional or unconscious discriminatory evaluations of racial/ethnic minority individuals because of underlying anxiety about race and ethnicity—termed aversive racism. Social role stereotypes of gender and race have also been found to influence the performance of women and racial/ethnic minorities. Steele (1997) found that these individuals might also underperform in situations where they are evaluated on a domain in which they are regarded, based on stereotypes, as inferior—termed stereotyped threat.

Evaluations of leaders often include characteristics associated with leaders and leadership but have little to do with effectiveness. Given that white males have typically occupied leadership positions, evaluations of leader effectiveness often favor male characteristics of height, white, and masculinity. Consequently, the context of masculinized norms and the expectations about what a leader looks like introduce conditions of bias against women and racial/ethnic minority leaders. It raises challenges that are not faced by white Anglo males.

Credible leadership reflects these concerns about the image, and in the advice to dress for success. While this applies to men and women, one's appearance and behavior may project unleader-like images and perceptions associated with gender and ethnicity that may have little to do with leadership. It is more complex for women since they tend to be defined by their external attributes and fashion. What they wear could be a distraction or fit stereotypic images of being too feminine or too ethnic, and therefore, not leader-like. Another challenge to credibility is the communication styles of women who tend to have softer, high-pitched voices which may be perceived as being less commanding than a loud, booming male voice. This is reflected in the common observation of their being ignored or not being yielded the floor to speak by others, and becomes a way to disempower women.

Performance appraisals of women are evaluated more negatively compared to men even when performing the same leadership behaviors. There is bias against women leaders in appraisals of their effectiveness and expectations of their leader behaviors (Eagly & Carli, 2007). This often places them in double-bind situations when they feel compelled to conform to different role expectations associated with gender and leadership. Are they to be feminine women and be perceived as weak, or strong leaders to be perceived as too domineering? Whereas current organizations typically conform to masculinized norms more congruent for men, women leaders can be at a disadvantage when exercising behaviors that contradict such expectations or when they are compelled to conform to these norms.

MULTIPLE AND INTERSECTION IDENTITIES

Contemporary theories of leadership endorse authenticity in leaders—in knowing who they are, what they believe and value (Avolio, Gardner, Walumbwa, Luthans, & May 2004, p. 803). Avolio (2007) calls for the level of integration in leadership theory and research which considers the dynamic interplay between leaders and followers, taking into account the prior, current, and emerging context in explaining what improves or develops leadership—he called this authentic leadership development. While theories of leadership would have us believe that gender and ethnicity are inconsequential to leadership, it is increasingly clear that cultural worldviews, socialization of gender roles, and different life experiences do contribute to one's resulting philosophy and style of leadership. Authenticity as a leader is more challenging when needing to negotiate multiple and intersecting identities. Women from diverse racial and ethnic groups might lead in different ways more aligned with their different world views and cultural perspectives. They may identify not only as leaders but also as women, as racial/ethnic individuals, as mothers, etc., all of which intersect with one another. These include the challenges of work-family balance, caretaking responsibilities, gender role expectations, connectedness, and affiliation with multiple communities while exercising their leadership.

As the literature on gender differences in leadership has shown, it is often not the differences in what women and racial/ethnic minority leaders do in their enactment of leadership as much as it is the different experiences they face when they lead. Given the tendency to view traits held by women and racial/ethnic minority groups as negative or deficient because they are viewed as exceptions or different, leadership is a different experience.

In Women and Leadership (Chin, Lott, Rice & Sanchez-Hucles, 2007), they examined leadership among more than 100 feminist women leaders. While many preferred a feminist leadership style that was more collaborative and inclusive, many felt this was not sanctioned within the institutions they led. Many feminist women often sought leadership positions to achieve social justice goals, striving to be transformational in their vision, empowering in their actions, and upholding ethical principles. These principles often were felt to be at odds with strivings for power and status more commonly associated with men. Many of the women felt constrained to follow institutional rules defined by masculinized norms and needing to compromise feminist principles in their leadership styles to be effective.

When we factor in diversity including issues of race, ethnicity, ability status, and sexual orientation, the exercise of leadership becomes more complex. We need to move beyond single dimensions of identity in our theorizing, and instead investigate multiple and intersecting identities if we are to obtain a more comprehensive understanding of how diversity contributes to important phenomena such as leadership (Chin & Sanchez-Hucles, 2007). Case examples suggest that an African American woman may identify with the values of straightforwardness and assertiveness in their leadership style while an Asian American woman may identify with values of respectfulness and unobtrusiveness. However, others may perceive the direct confrontational style of an African American woman as intimidating and deem the use of an indirect teaching style of an Asian American woman as passive. These factors are likely to influence access to leadership positions and appraisals of their effectiveness as leaders.

Hall, Garrett-Akinsanya, & Hucles (2007, p. 283) define Black feminist leaders as: Black activists who, from the intersections of race and gender, develop paths, provide a direction, and give a voice to Black women. Kawahara, Esnil, & Hsu (2007, p. 310), in their interviews, found that Asian American women leaders held a collectivistic view of their leadership styles, and used bicultural values to achieve their leadership goals. Native American women described their leadership as stand[ing] besides, rather than behind, [their] men in their effort to preserve their tribes and treaty rights (Kidwell, Willis, Jones-Saumty, & Bigfoot, 2007, p. 327). They will not distance themselves from their men because of the inherent threat posed by broader society against their men if they were to distance themselves. These case examples need further investigation but suggest different leadership styles influenced by cultural differences.

Lorene Garrett-Browder suggests that African American women throughout history have been able to be effective leaders despite living in an oppressive environment and dealing with power structures that do not always include our voice. Consequently, African American women leaders might tend to use more direct communication styles and have used our anger as an ally to help us speak the truth ... even though it may be unpopular. In a context of oppression and power, value is placed on trust and fairness to accept leadership from an African American perspective. This approach emphasizes parity and social justice.

Ann Yabusaki suggests that Asian American women may use more indirect communication in their leadership styles. In Asian cultures, the balance of opposites and emphasis on the yin and the yang can bring out the best in leadership enriched by different perspectives. She identifies how the emphasis on hierarchy influences ways in which leaders and authority figures communicate in Asian cultures, resulting in the expectation and tendency of Asian leaders to teach or convey a moral message when communicating. When this communication operates within a context that values kinship bonds and elders, the concept of benevolent authority is ascribed to leaders in the Asian culture.

These examples suggest that diverse women leaders may hold different views about assertiveness and express their leadership in different ways. Yet, their competence and effectiveness as leaders may be defined by social role stereotypes and expectations. Asian American women may need to learn how to toot one's horn without losing one's modesty or to speak up, although the Asian culture values listening. Native American women may need to learn how to get a seat at the table, and not wait to be asked. The challenge for diverse women leaders is to learn that it is a different game governed by different rules while transforming the organizational culture in the process.

TOWARD MORE ROBUST LEADERSHIP THEORIES

The growing population diversity and more permeable borders in our global society demand attention to how women and diverse leaders are included in our models of leadership. Books on leadership have generally viewed them as special populations while leadership studies remain silent. It is increasingly clear that a race and gender-neutral view of leadership fails to consider the influence of cultural worldviews and socialization on shaping leadership style. Defining and understanding leadership by simply examining those who currently hold leadership positions has led to a biased and incomplete portrayal of leadership and leader effectiveness. Whereas the experiences of women and diverse leaders may be different, these differences may serve to expand the world views reflected in existing leadership theories. What follows are ways to incorporate gender and diversity into our leadership theories.

TRAIT THEORIES

Trait theory, assumes behavior is determined by stable traits which are fundamental sectors of one's personality. Traits indicate a predisposition to act in one certain way, regardless of the situation. Traits are often measured by psychometric tests (McLeod, 2021).

Although trait theory fell by the wayside, leadership traits and attributes do matter according to Zaccaro (2007) who argues that combinations of traits and attributes are more likely to predict leadership. Yet, it is not clear how and if the range of traits now studied are representative of those manifested by diverse leaders or simply that of Anglo males who are now in the majority as leaders. Nor is it clear how these traits are confounded by biases based on social role expectations. Most studies using trait theories have not examined the intersection of race/ethnicity, gender, or other dimensions of diversity with leadership traits. For example, studies of charismatic leadership have focused on characteristics more aligned with masculine traits. Whereas trait theories often see leadership characteristics as innate, (e.g., "born leaders"), they fail to consider the influence of social/environmental factors which have precluded women and racial/ethnic groups from such positions.

Trait theories have not considered concept equivalence across cultures when measuring attributes or traits. Assertiveness defined along one dimension may find women deficient; expanding it to include that different expressions may eliminate those differences between men and women. Diverse leaders have different experiences which may influence how they lead in different contexts even when all other factors are held constant. It is not uncommon to measure these traits using bipolar dimensions (e.g., assertive vs. passive; task-oriented vs. interpersonal) this may result in canceling out differences than if each were rated independently.

CONTINGENCY THEORIES

Contingency or situational leadership theory offers an alternative approach to the problems posed by trait theories since it proceeds from the assumption that different situations call for different leadership characteristics; accordingly, there is no single profile of a leader. Contingency theories examine contexts and situations, and the interaction of leadership behavior and characteristics with follower characteristics. While these lend themselves to including the complexities of diversity, the context of leadership in these studies is typically the organizational culture in which leadership is exercised. A broader definition of contexts to include the cultural and social contexts would be more robust especially as we begin to look at the exercise of leadership within a global context and diverse society.

EMPOWERMENT AND SHARED LEADERSHIP

Leadership implies a relationship of power, the power to guide others. David McClelland (1975) studied the psychology of power and achievement and saw leadership skills not so much as a set of traits but as a pattern of motives. Emphasis on power has fallen into disfavour with a shift from power to empowerment where the leader places power in one's followers. Emerging leadership models have shifted from distinguishing authoritarian vs democratic leadership styles (more common post World War II) to shared power and the servant leader as characteristic styles of the modern leader. The research has not yet examined how the use of power by leaders is mediated by race, ethnicity, gender, and disability status. For example, feminist leaders tend to prioritize social justice motives over power motives to seek leadership positions. Nor has the research examined how more collaborative and collective cultures might influence the exercise of leadership. For example, businesses internationally have begun to shift from merely adopting Western theories and practices of management to cherishing unique social and cultural factors inherent in non-Western cultures while revising Western management theories (Kao, Sinha, & Wilpert, 1999).

LEADERSHIP STYLE

Leadership theories often reflect the larger social contexts in which they were developed. Leadership studies post World War II, for example, emphasizing top-down, command and control models of leadership style, have shifted toward more collaborative and transformational models given the rapid social and technological changes of today's global society. Leadership studies shifted from examining autocratic vs democratic styles of leadership to transformational vs transactional styles of leadership. Emerging models of leadership are now more value-driven, ethics-based, and social change-oriented in response to the fallout from such events as the Enron scandal symbolizing willful corporate fraud and corruption, the banking industry's financial crisis, and the collapse of the housing and dot.com bubble during the beginning of the twenty-first century.

James MacGregor Burns (1978) defined transformational leadership as a process where leaders and followers engage in a mutual process of raising one another to higher levels of morality and motivation and introduced the concept of the shared vision that unites leaders and followers toward a common purpose. Many definitions of leadership involve vision, providing direction, influencing the process, orienting toward achieving a future desired state, and energizing followers. This has been central to transformational leadership styles and requires the leader to communicate that vision to followers to embrace as their own. Increasingly, transformational leadership styles are endorsed as essential for today's leaders given its emphasis on defining leadership as a process concerned with fostering change. It is intentional, directed toward a future end or condition, is a purposive process, and inherently value-based. How much changing demographics in the workplace contributed to this shift is a question.

CONTEXT OF HIGHER EDUCATION

Higher education plays a major role in shaping the quality of leadership in today's society. Today's rapidly changing and diverse global society are mirrored in our institutions of higher education and present challenges to how we prepare and educate students today to be the leaders of tomorrow. Transformational leadership is a model consistent with the goals of higher education today, whose purpose is to enable and encourage faculty, students, administrators, and other staff to change and transform institutions to more effectively enhance student learning, generate new knowledge, and empower students to become agents of positive social change in the larger society.

However, institutions of higher education are organized along with two contradictory sets of practices. First, the administrative hierarchy is generally top-down; budgets at the chair level within these institutions often have limited discretionary spending with personnel (which makes up the bulk of budgets) generally controlled by administration. At the same time, faculty who forms the bottom rungs of this hierarchy with less or little power also has great power because of tenure, unions, and principles of academic freedom. As a result, faculty operates with a great deal of autonomy in their primary work of teaching and research.

Tenure and professional status within current institutions of higher education are structured to be individualistic. Contrary to egalitarian and collective systems, current organizational structures in higher education institutions breed competitiveness for funding, the brightest students, and attracting top faculty. Peer review, a potential mechanism for collegial and collaborative leadership may be derailed by faculty who see themselves exclusively as critics to judge rather than as colleagues to offer constructive feedback or by those with personal agendas viewing potential promotions as threats or competitors.

This hierarchical approach within higher education sits alongside the faculty committee structure, which is more collegial. The typical committee is often advisory with little leadership responsibility; products and recommendations need to be vetted up the line. While committees offer possibilities for collegial or collaborative leadership, leadership opportunities may not always be realized.

REFERENCE

Janice Bryant Howard is an African American multimillionaire entrepreneur and philanthropist. To many surprise, she is the first woman to own a billion-dollar business. Her company generates $1.1 billion in net sales which makes her one of the richest self-made women in America.

Starting her business with a $1,500 and little entrpreneueal experience along with being a Black woman, statistically places her at a disadvantage. However, with her work ethic, innovative style and relentless determination she was able to have others believe in her business giving her a chance to showcase her skills, perfect her business skills and expand.

Janice's quote of 'determination, belief in yourself and ethical resilience' serves me well every day. Whatever position I hold as a team member or as the President of my two companies, I always embrace determination and resilience. There is just no other way.

She mananged and expanded her business on a grassroot principle of never compromising her personal self for her professional self (Connley, 2018).

THE TAKEAWAY

You don't have to start a business with a large sum of money. What makes women leaders flourish is exhibiting innovation and determination. Women leaders have unique challenges that cause them to figure out creative ways to manage their businesses and careers. You can have all of the investment financing that one can dream of but without determination, belief in yourself or the ability to do things in a way that is ethically resilient you will find yourself in an unstatainable situation. You will not always see someone else in the seat that you are looking to fill and that is okay. There are so many opportunities for women of color to be "firsts" and to break the glass.

As an entrepreneur, you are truly the painter of your own mosaic. Meaning, if you decide not to get your supplies and paint, your canvas will remain blank. In business, if you don't create opportunities, generate streams of income, build relationships and follow through on client deliverables daily, you will have no clients ... along with an empty bank account. You must take steps every day to drive towards the outcomes you envision.

One quote that gets me through my toughest days is from Elizabeth Taylor: "you just do it. You force yourself to get up. You force yourself to put one foot before the other, and God damn it, you refuse to let it get to you. You fight. You cry. You curse. Then you go about the business of living. That's how I've done it. There's no other way."

THE BENEFITS OF STAMINA

You want to be in this for the long haul and not burn out. That requires stamina. We may get excited about an opportunity and then burn the candle at both ends but fail to keep the pace when we finally land the job, position, or career we worked so hard to attain. Impactful leaders understand that burn out isn't the way to maintain long term success. How many LinkedIn posts have I read from women, who thought constant work was the way to achieve their professional goals only to later realize that regardless of their professional goals being met or not, they had grossly sacrificed some facet of their life: their personal relationships, friendships, health, peace, mind and or physical health.

As women, it is mandatory that we take care of our entire physical being: mind, body and spirit. As a flight attendant, I repeated the safety message several times, "Put on your oxygen mask first before helping others." At twenty-one, I didn't think much of it outside of the context of flying but it's imperative in life as well. You can't take care of anyone else if your oxygen tank is depleted. However, women often don't embrace this practice, instead we put ourselves last, skipping critical, yet routine medical check-ups, postponing our workouts, not finding the time to seek therapy, canceling connection meetings with friends and extended family, and the list goes on. We believe that we are helping others when we behave in this way when it is the opposite. If you are exhausted and unfocused with unresolved baggage, this can spill over to your kid's lives: how you engage with them, react to them, advice you provide, your patience level, etc. In addition, children know when you aren't fully present, they pick up your energy. The same with your partners; you may respond with irritation, dispondence, or anger at situtions that under normal circumstances wouldn't warrant that reaction.

After reading this, don't beat yourself up about where you are now. This is to bring awarness to the importance of self-care and being cognizant of behaviors that have been on autopilot for years.

Effective leaders know the value of protecting their health on and off the job. In fact, according to an article called "Daily Habits of the World's Most Successful CEOs" on *BusinessInsider.com*: "Regular exercise is almost as common among successful CEOs as getting up early. This is one of the first things that many of these professionals incorporate in the day. Andrea Jung, the former CEO of Avon Products, always got up at 5:00 am to use the gym before work."

SIX TIPS FOR STAMINA

Most CEOs, in my experience, believe that fitness, discipline, and nutrition are important to them. But, to put in the type of long hours that leadership requires, you need to know how to deal with stress. To do that, and so much more, here are six handy tips:

1. Focus on wellness

Believe it or not, many women I talk to have gone years without so much as a single wellness checkup. This includes women of all ages. As we know, women are being diagnosed with chronic illnesses in their twenties and thirtees that are customary for women in their fiftees. Beginning with your annual physical is optimal and then ensuring you have annual mammograms, gynecological, optical exams. Getting into the habit of regular checkups as well as simple diagnostics that can help measure and regulate your blood pressure, cholesterol, nutrition, weight, and even energy which all plays a role in how focused you can be on achieving your personal and professional dreams.

2. Move your body

Bar none, the first, middle, and the last thing you can do to increase your stamina—which is like fuel for your journey from competence to confidence—is simply to move more and more often. Physical activity releases endorphins, the "feel good" substances in our bodies, making us happier as a result. When we feel better, we do better, and the best way to feel better is to begin moving regularly before, during, and after work. Please don't conflate moving your body with weight loss. They are not the same. Physical exercise is a testament to your physical health and maintenace and not for weight loss which requires a different regimen.

3. Delegate

Believe it or not, one of the things we hear women say is that they have a hard time finding the energy to do all they need to do simply because they have so much on their plates! According to the U.S. Department of Labor during the height of the COVID-19 pandemic, more than 2 million women dropped out of the labor force between February 2020 and October 2020, leaving the lowest percentage of working women in over thirthy years. This was largely because women are the caregivers for their families. The good news is remedies exist. The onset and growth of the gig economy has opened up a new era with Fiverr, UpWork and virtual assistants that are available from around the globe willing and able to complete simple to more complex tasks.

4. Practice self-care

You can't appear confident, let alone have the stamina if you're not practicing some form of daily self-care. Do what works for you, what relaxes you, and what prepares you for your journey. Take a walk, take a sauna, sleep well, take a bath, see a movie, go to a concert, read a book, take a class, write in a gratitude journal, seek therapy, enjoy a staycation or extended weekend or literally stop and smell the roses—but make self-care as much of a priority in your personal life as self-preservation is in your professional life. You simply can't have one without the other.

Arianna Huffington, co-founder of *The Huffington Post* and CEO of Thrive Global, and the author of fifteen books and *Time Magazine*'s list of the world's 100 most influential people along with Forbes Most Powerful Women list, came home from work in 2007 and collapsed from sleep deprivation and burnout, hitting the floor leaving a visible scar on her head, a broken cheekbone and a ride to the hospital. She found her solice in gratitude, disconnecting from the digital world and removing things and people from your life that are not helpful.

About 25 percent of people spend more time on their phones than they actually spend sleeping (Diaz, 2021).

5. Make it a team effort

If self-care is difficult for you, enlist accountability partners to join together as you all learn to take care of one another. We can't make it alone in this life. We need others to make life complete, but also to make life better. The more we share with others, the more we learn about ourselves. And when you surround yourself with happy, friendly, positive people, you will find yourself more energized to face the task(s) at hand. For those that are excellent at holding others accountable, becoming an accountability coach is a growing career.

6. Enjoy yourself

I think a big part of stamina is having fun and joy in your life. Working with fun people, having a pleasant work environment, and learning to laugh at—and with—yourself and others immediately lowers your stress and allow you to feel better for longer, increasing your stamina while having fun!

THE TAKEAWAY

As women, we often put everyone else first: on the job, at home, and everywhere in between. Until we learn to practice self-care, stamina will always be an issue for us. But remember, you can't get all you need to be for everyone in your life if you don't take care of yourself first.

Even sprinters have to train for weeks and months at a time, even if it's just for a short burst that takes less than a minute to run. Leaders are no different from athletes. Suppose we want to complete the journey from competence to confidence and perform at the highest level. In that case, we must prepare accordingly and take pains to stay in good health, emotionally and physically, to ensure that we are able to maintain high energy and performance day in, day out, time and time again.

Too many of us try to shine so brightly, so often, that we burn out before we reach our peak potential. Settle in for the long haul and rise to the occasion when needed, but do your best to separate work and life so that you can embrace the benefits of balance.

It took me a while to figure out meritocracy was indeed a myth. For a long time, I believed the person with the most passion, most deliverables and greatest outcomes would naturally win. I figured out over time that this isn't the case. There are so many other factors that weigh into building a positive career trajectory. Stamina alone will not positively impact your career. It's being organizationally savvy, building relationships, the ability to distinguish sponsors from mentors, the foresight to know your worth and to walk with confidence regardless of what you feel others are thinking. Meanwhile, as a woman, and for me as a woman of colour, it's necessary to understand that others are judging you based on their own belief system and stereotypes. I have never been one to try and disprove what I feel someone thinks about me, because that is a losing prophecy you will not win or control. You will never have the ability to control someone else's frame of thinking, their unique biases and what environmental factors cultivated their thought process.

DRAFTING YOUR WINNING TEAM

As the famous saying goes, "No-one succeeds in this life alone." It's easy to become focused on building the various facets of our lives that include our families, spouses, partners, friends, families, career, educational and philanthropic endeavors, that we forget that our lives could be so much easier if we embraced the notion of drafting a winning team. I have coached women at various stages in their careers that don't fully embrace this concept or have any idea of the impact that a winning team has in every facet of your life, and more specifically, your career.

When we think of drafting a winning team, sports comes to mind. When the NFL or the NBA drafts, millions worldwide watch to see which team will draft the best and brightest with the most potential. The process is generally a lottery that gives teams the best position in the lottery and an advantage in determining the talent selection for their team. It's a laborious and arduous process that the entire league takes seriously because the objective is to select the players that will give your team a winning advantage over the other teams in the league.

Therefore, why don't we have the same concept regarding our careers? We need to surround ourselves with people that will help us win. A team committed has diverse strengths, opinions, and backgrounds, and has navigated the storm in various functional areas, geographies, and types of organizations.

Most professionals only have access to an executive coach once they are well into their careers, generally at the director level and above. Can you imagine your career trajectory with several individuals coaching you to become the best version of yourself?

However, we continue to tread the beaten path alone or with limited perspectives and resources.

As this chapter courageously states, there are concepts for drafting your winning team.

Elise Awwad, the chief operating officer at DeVry University, stated, "For many women working in the business world, finding a trusted personal board of advisors is one way to support growth and progress. I have found it helpful to have a focused group of personal advisors who know me well and share my fundamental values," (LinkedIn, July 2021).

Elise has not only practiced this throughout her career but has also refined the process as she advanced over the past ten years.

A personal board of directors can help in many ways, including:

- Looking at a situation through a different lens, one that you may not have considered.
- Making you aware of blind spots.
- Challenging your thinking to embrace another perspective or solution.
- Highlighting your strengths and encouraging you to move forward or reconsider a decision not aligning with your overall

career goals and trajectory.

Drafting your winning team is comprised of assigning the correct position to the right player. For instance, you wouldn't place Russell Wilson, the NFL's top quarterback, into an offensive tackle position, not because he couldn't perform in that role but because it would not be the best use of his talents. We employ the same strategy in drafting and building our winning advisory team.

As seriously as the National Basketball League, National Football League, Major League Baseball, and National Soccer Leagues own the responsibility to select, coach, develop, encourage, and position their players to win, we must draft our winning team with the same vivaciousness, consideration, calculation, and foreshadowing.

Now that we understand this is a critical step in our development and career journey, it's equally important to understand the various positions.

Mentors share their knowledge, expertise, and career path with you. They often provide emotional support, resources, and assistance in helping you create a plan to achieve your career goals based on their experiences.

Executive coach generally has either a one-on-one executive coaching relationship or a cohort of leaders that focuses on increasing the self-awareness of the client's thoughts, behaviors, and actions and the leader's impact on the team.

Leadership coach helps you become a better version of yourself, ultimately transforming you into a more impactful leader.

According to Elise Awwad, COO at DeVry University, to be a member of a **personal board of advisors,** members must be vested interest in your success. Still, you should also vet members based on their strengths with the understanding that your board will 'morph over time as we change and grow".

A sponsor is someone that has more career capital than you. They are in a higher position, have more influence, and can directly impact your career. Sponsors are talking about you in rooms where you are absent. They advocate for your career in ways that could lead to a promotion, stretch assignment, visibility on an important strategic project, access to coaching, or involvement in strategy sessions. They are your voice amongst individuals with whom you rarely interact.

A connector networks make viable and relevant professional connections for you. They have an innate ability to connect you with others that can be a resource to you.

As you read through the various positions, you can see it's imperative to have a diversity of players on your team for enhanced career perspective, development, and direction.

Now that we know who should be members of our team, there are methods where women can support one another in the workplace and ways that men can support women in the workplace.

HOW CAN WOMEN ADVOCATE FOR ONE ANOTHER IN THE WORKPLACE?

1. Make sure one another's ideas are heard – men successfully navigate being heard because they tend to sit in seats that garner more attention, which tend to be the front-and-center seats in meetings. Other women can be examples by sitting front and center and communicating their thoughts in discussions.
2. Celebrate each other's accomplishments – we must amplify one another's successes at work and personal achievements.
3. Encourage women to take on a new role or project if they are

suffering from imposter syndrome or self-doubt when they are more than qualified to succeed in a new career endeavor.

4. Provide constructive feedback to women that is unbiased and addresses career-derailing behaviors or tactics that will help elevate a women's perceived leadership.
5. Although women are often stretched in terms of mentoring and sponsoring one other, we must continue to do so on an unleveled playing field. Diligence before accepting an opportunity to mentor or sponsor someone will help you preserve your energy. Aligning with a mentee who is not fully engaged and despondent will cause exhaustion and hesitancy from a mentor with the bandwidth to help others. (leanin.org, 2023)

Men, you are not off the hook! Ultimately, we must all support one another in the workplace, irrespective of gender. Therefore, here are ways in which men can also help their counterparts in the workplace:

MEN SUPPORTING WOMEN IN THE WORKPLACE

1. Give credit where credit is due. When women's ideas are hijacked in meetings, speak up and give the originator credit for her contribution.
2. Invite women to off-site social events. We know much work-related information is shared during off-site social activities. Not inviting women and people of color to these events is an undue disadvantage to those that were not invited. Don't assume women wouldn't want to golf or participate because of personal responsibilities.
3. Ensure your team is diverse, and if not, change it!

4. Champion for equity in compensation for women. According to the United States Department of Labor, women earn .82 cents for every $1 a man earns. According to the Time and the Bureau of Labor Statistics, women aged sixteen to seventy will earn $590,000 less than men who work the same time span. This impacts not only women but men as well. (time.com/5562269/equal-pay-day-women-men-lifetime-wages)
5. Actively listen and no mansplaining. When you actively listen, you will recognize someone's understanding versus jumping to mansplaining. Mansplaining is when men explain something to a woman condescendingly, assuming she has no knowledge about the topic. (Merriam-Webster.) This behavior can have detrimental outcomes in the workplace, making women seem incompetent or unprepared.

Once again, we are the CEOs of our careers and must act accordingly, but this doesn't absolve others of the critical role they play in women's careers. It takes a village to build your career and the careers of others. We must support one another's successes, ambitions, and dreams. Organizational culture and financial stability suffer when the ecosystem is not equitable and respectful for all.

REPUTATION

Think of your reputation as the echo that lingers in the room long after you leave. In fact, it's also what precedes you into the room, a kind of subconscious energy or presence you carry around with you wherever you go. For me, "reputation" and "brand" are nearly interchangeable. Each is a reflection of your executive leadership presence.

Many people think they know what their reputations are. Some are right, while others are way off base. People in the organization actually think about us because it affects how they make decisions about us. It can even affect how much exposure we're getting in the organization and whether or not people want to sponsor us for various leadership opportunities that arise.

If you have a reputation as a dependable, trustworthy, and discreet person, then people are far more willing to share information, access, and opportunities. If you develop a reputation as someone with fickle allegiances and loyalties or with a mean streak, then you may find opportunities closed off to you.

Reputations don't exist in a vacuum. Quite often, the way we are perceived—our personal brand—is tied to our relationship with others and how they are perceived. We need to be careful about the workplace alliances we make and be sure that they are advantageous to our brand as well as our career.

Many leaders are afraid to know how they are actually perceived. They rarely get feedback from their bosses on areas where they need to improve, especially when they move into the organization. Yet, it is vitally important that they know how they are viewed to continue improving and growing. I have implemented, and been the recipient, in many organizations to what is commonly referenced as a 360-degree feedback tool. This is meant to provide a 360-degree view of your leadership style and effectiveness from team members at various levels in the workplace. For many women, this was the first time they received professional feedback.

THE TAKEAWAY

As we move forward through the next section, think critically about your brand and how eager people are to work with you. If your brand needs fixing, you will find tools here for that. And even if your brand is already strong, you will find tools to help you make it even stronger.

RECOGNIZING YOUR OWN ABILITIES

One aspect of being competent but not confident is underselling, even underappreciating, our own personal skills related to our brand or reputation. Perhaps because we feel we can't be our authentic selves at work, we neglect to offer the intense value inherent in what we alone can bring to the workplace equation.

THE REAL

The big message in all of this is what I call The Real, which is when a woman's **Reinvention** is **Aligned** with her **Energy** and **Livelihood,** when a woman's confidence and competence connect to each to serve all aspects of her life well. At ReimagineOD as well as in my coaching practice, The Executive Women of Command, I work with women who are not newcomers in their careers; they have been working for fifteen to twenty-five years, and they don't suffer from a lack of intelligence, know-how, experience, or even opportunity.

Leading is not about making them smarter but about recognizing their worth. One of the things I see quite often is that women don't tend to raise their hands and ask for the chance to step up, lead, and perform. They know they are more than capable, and yet time and time again, when presented with an opportunity, they don't step up and ask for the assignment. So we see that there is a gap between a woman's ability (competence) and showing up and raising her hand (confidence).

My ultimate goal for writing this book is to inspire women to find how to be REAL and understand the assignment. I want to help the woman who possesses competency and proficiency in her work, someone who shows up, is dedicated, understands what is necessary but is simply not being forthcoming about her career aspirations because she is not asking for the promotion that she deserves or raising her hand for a project that is going to give her the necessary visibility to move on and upward with the organization, or forming the pitch necessary to obtain the capital that is needed for her business. The key for women is we all need to plant the seeds in everyone's garden for what we want even when we haven't been asked to plant it. This way, once an opportunity arises and you have made your career objectives clear you will at a minimum be considered, whereas without being clear about your direction you are leaving your fate in the hands of someone else. Women need to understand that they can start today, right where they are. They can speak up, they can be their own advocates, and they can recognize their own value and carry that into the next meeting, conversation, initiative, or project.

According to the research firm McKinsey & Company, 83 percent of women currently in middle management positions desire to move to the next level at work, while more than 50 percent say it's essential for them to have a leadership role in the organization. So the gap between women and leadership isn't coming from them not being interested. Perhaps it could be that they are not letting people know they are interested.

For many women, this is the place where confidence could be getting them to the next level—and insecurity is keeping them back. Ellen East of Time Warner explains, "I really do think it's all about being comfortable. I think if you are comfortable with who you are and how you're presenting yourself to the world, then you will be confident."

So leveraging your personal skills is about recognizing that you are as capable—or even more capable—than the people around you. I read an article once that said that if a job is posted in an organization and there are ten qualifications listed for getting it, a woman will read those ten items and say, "Well, I don't have what they're asking for. I only have eight and so I am not going to apply for this job." Yet for the very same position, and those very same ten qualifications, a man may say, "Well, I only have three, and I am totally going to get this job!"

Now, just doing the simple math here, if every woman who doubted herself over having just eight qualifications showed up anyway, one of them would most likely get the job over those confident guys who might have only three qualifications. But if you never show up, guess who's getting the job ... every time? Not every time, but certainly much of the time.

In talking about the difference between how men show up at work versus how women show up, Vernice "FlyGirl" Armour, points out, "Guys are more vocal about their stuff. A woman may be confident in her job and what she's doing. She'll keep her head down and work and think, 'I'm working super hard. I'm going to get rewarded. They're going to promote me. They're going to see how hard I'm working.' And she's confident in what she's doing. But guys are just going to talk about it. You know, he's going to voice what he wants and will be confident in voicing that."

Obviously, there is a difference between how we think about our own abilities and how that affects us asking for additional assignments and opportunities.

Confidence is comprised of believing that you have what it takes and having the audacity to go after it.

LEVERAGING WHAT MAKES YOU

I honestly don't think we can separate our personal and professional skills because, quite often, they tend to be the same. Whoever we are, whatever we're like, at home and with our friends, at a party or at a ballgame, we tend to bring all of those things with us to the workplace.

For example, if you are detail-oriented at home—very organized and thorough—then you are naturally going to be detail-oriented for the rest of your life as well. It may even be what got you hired in the first place, so why deny it? If you are relationship-centric at home—a people person who enjoys socializing and befriending and conversing and sharing—you are naturally going to bring those things to your organization.

We do ourselves a disservice when we try to parse out one way at work and another way at home. The skills we have in each place translate to the other parts of our lives. Whenever I see someone "transform" who she is the minute she walks into work, it makes me wonder how effective she is at her job because, after all, who she is is often what makes her so effective in the first place.

Of course, you may use your skills differently at work, but they are very much the same skills. For instance, creative people are creative everywhere they go. They're idea people. They can't help themselves.

If you're highly creative, you likely think of ways to solve problems, even when they aren't yours to solve. You think Oprah can bite her tongue with friends, acquaintances, strangers, guests, or coworkers if she's inspired to tell them something that will help them? Ideas are in her blood and have helped her achieve success.

Conversely, if you're more of a reflective or introverted person, you will bring those same qualities to your work role as well. Both relationship-centric skills and detail-oriented skills have value—perhaps not in the same role, but at least in some capacity. The same extroverted, relationship-centric skills that make one individual such a successful salesperson may wreak havoc in the accounting department, which tends to be populated by folks required to work in a more detail-oriented, reserved environment.

BE YOURSELF ... WITH GUARDRAILS

That said, it's essential to, as I say, be yourself ... but with guardrails. In other words, you're not in your living room. You're in your workplace, so you do have to temper your behavior and fit your environment. Your company is not your family. There are times when you will have to make decisions about adult behavior in your work environment.

This can affect how you:

- Communicate concerns. Are you going to voice every concern? Every time? And to whom? Are you going to rant and rave if you don't get your way? Or will you be mature and find a more appropriate, professional solution?
- Show up when the team is struggling. Are you going to pitch in even when it's someone else's fault? Or are you going to say, "It's not my responsibility" and go home at 5:00 anyway? Will you show humility and grace? Or will you hog the spotlight?

- Express yourself in terms of disappointment. Are you going to pout, fume, and blame others for your lack of progress? Are you going to go over your superior's head and try to garner favor with her superior? Or will you consider the fact that you may have fallen short—and then acquire the skills you need to avoid that shortcoming next time?
- Conduct yourself in social environments. Are you going to let it all hang out? Be "one of the boys" and forgo all propriety? Or will you have fun but still be sensible?
- Share information. Are you going to be careless with gossip and rumors? Are you going to act like you're in the high school halls, informing on a "frenemy" or picking sides with the "cool kids"? Or will you remember that you're in the workplace and value the art of discretion?

When you're at a work-related function, you're not "off the clock." You are always making an impression on the organization. If you are a super social partier—the kind of person who has one too many glasses of wine at a client event or too many beers at the work-sponsored softball game—it affects your brand. You're there to have fun, not to be a social-media poster child. I promise you, these days, one racy or inappropriate smartphone photo of you making a wrong choice at a company party, and all the confidence and competence in the world won't help you recover.

I have seen many young women make the mistake of thinking that after-hours events, parties, and social interaction with people from work don't matter throughout my career. It does. And, increasingly, so does what you post on your Facebook page or in your Twitter feed and other forms of social media. You may think, "It's my personal life and none of the company's business," but if you want to be looked at as a leader and someone who is going places in an organization, then you want to be aware of how you're showing up even when you're not at the office.

If your brand is essential to you (and it should be), you have to be very careful about the decisions you make and how much you "relax" in work-related social environments. The same eyes that watch you during board meetings or conference calls are watching you at the employee picnic, cookout, after-work happy hour, ballgame, and convention after-party.

You must know that while alcohol is part of many work-related events, it is not your friend. I have had to release a HR executive, several senior managers, and far more rank-and-file employees than I cared to because they acted out at after-hours events to the point where it didn't just hurt their brand but could have affected the organization's brand as well.

When you are with work colleagues, your reputation is always on the clock. This includes what you say in a voicemail, in an email, or a text message. Nothing is private anymore; you must be very thoughtful about how you "show up" in person, online, and electronic communications. If you have specific personal qualities that make you successful, they will probably help you be successful at work. But keep in mind that any muscle overused becomes a weakness.

THE TAKEAWAY

The REAL—when a woman's (R)einvention is (A)ligned with her (E)nergy and (L)ivelihood—as I mentioned at the beginning of this chapter, is the sweet spot where your reinvention maps to your essence. They're not mutually exclusive, so you won't hear or feel the

REAL with only executing one component but not the others. So, for instance, if you are only leaning on the fact that "Gee, I am a great relationship builder," but you are not getting things done, or you are really high on execution, but nobody in the organization knows who you are, then you're fully being REAL.

That's why my seven Rs of success are so effective in providing you with the tools you need to go from competence to confidence and then on to leadership. Only when you factor in relationships, reputation, results, resilience and reimagining will you get to the next leadership level. But take heart: We're halfway there!

BUILDING YOUR PERSONAL BRAND

Your personal brand is both a reflection of and an extension of you. The more purposeful you are about how you present your brand, the more powerful it will be.

THE EVOLUTION OF A PERSONAL BRAND

My brand evolved gradually over the years. Naturally, when I first began my career, I wanted to please and serve and grow and learn, which didn't allow for as much branding as I might have liked. As I grew in experience and position, as I began to get the lay of the land at each subsequent company where I worked, I could refine and enhance my brand to adapt to the organization and exert my influence over it.

Today I am seen as a risk-taker, powerful and confident, as someone who helps women become leaders and helps leaders become better leaders. I am seen as someone influential who can turn an idea into an actual outcome. I am seen as someone willing to help others and to hold them and myself accountable.

That inspires people to engage me because most people want problem solvers, not problem makers.

I am an extreme extrovert with some introverted qualities, better known as an ambivert. But because I am a storyteller and because I enjoy being in front of groups of people, I have become more comfortable being in front of others—so much that I work as a public speaker. Sometimes people are shocked to learn that I can equally enjoy a weekend at home as a night out on the town.

It's important to understand that self-awareness of what makes you good at what you do is also the self-awareness that makes you question yourself by saying things such as:

- "Hmmm, how do I make sure I am open to these other things?"
- "I am listening to others more now."
- "I do not have to be right all of the time."
- "I may not feel like being social, but networking is important to me."
- "Am I letting others share their ideas?"

Recently, I participated in an exercise with a group of ten people whom I had just met. Only a few minutes into the meeting, the facilitator had everyone do a "first impression" exercise. Each of us was asked to select four of the people we had just met and talk about our first impression of them by responding to the following: "List three reasons why you would want to work with this person and three reasons why you might not want to work with this person. And go!" Seven of the other ten participants decided to give me feedback. For starters, the positive things they listed when wanting to work with me were that they felt I was powerful, strong, direct, and professional. Interestingly, the negative things about me were the same as on the positive list! I thought this example was a perfect way to describe the decisions we make about people so quickly and about how our brands get communicated even when we haven't had much time to communicate. As a marketing friend of mine says, "Even when you're not intentionally marketing, your brand is communicating." Think about it, and you'll see that it is the same with your personal brand. People are ascribing qualities to you based on what they see when you show up.

"You can't take things personally," says Jill Campbell. "You have to learn from it and move on. It's vital to learn from feedback so you understand what went wrong or what you did that caused something to occur, but from then you have to shake it off and move on. And I think that makes you stronger because you know not to do something the next time around. That goes back to being very self-aware."

You have a brand, whether you manage it or not. Your brand and your reputation are interchangeable. How people see you and how they work with you, work for you, or even lead you are critically linked. There is an exercise I do in one of my workshops where I just start tossing out words like "lazy," "contradictive," and "negative." Then I ask the group, "Now, do any of your coworkers pop into your head when you hear those words?" Almost everyone immediately nods and smiles and says, "Yes."

Sadly, that is the brand of that person each workshop participant thought of. If that person were you, and enough people had begun to see you that way, your brand would have a direct impact on how effectively you did your job. And if your brand is negative enough, for long enough, it can seriously affect what happens in your career. That's why I want you to create a strong, powerful brand that's full of executive presence and courageous leadership.

To be honest, I've not been confident a day in my life. I guess that makes me kind of lucky as women go. So I don't have a story to share where I've never been confident. But I've certainly had moments of fear; I've had moments of not thinking that I could get where I wanted to go. Not because I didn't think I was capable, but perhaps there were other obstacles or things that I needed that I couldn't get or didn't have.

I think it's so essential for women to get the different layers of what makes us operate—and how we have to peel through those layers to get what we want.

The first way is to make sure you are surrounded by people who affirm you and speak positive things to and about who you are, what your gifts are, and how to manage them.

The second way you build confidence is to love yourself, respect yourself, know your value, and be significantly linked to who you know—who's talking to you, what they're saying to you, what they're saying about you. So, your confidence levels are really dependent on how much you think about yourself.

If you look at Oprah Winfrey, Arianna Huffington, and Michelle Obama, these are women who overcame significant obstacles. Oprah, for example, grew up very poor, her grandmother raised her, she'd been sexually abused, African American, not very attractive by her own admission, and overweight, right? So, if you look at Oprah, everything in Oprah's surroundings of life told her she would be unsuccessful. Black female at a time—you know, she's sixty years old, Oprah grew up in a civil rights era context.

So everything in Oprah's world would've told her she couldn't succeed. But Oprah has said many times that the reason she succeeded is that somewhere deep inside, she knew she was destined to do something great with her life. She knew she was meant to be more than the roles that were allocated to Black women at the time, but yet she still succeeded.

Michelle Obama grew up on the South Side of Chicago in a modest home, with her brother, mom, and dad. And went to Princeton, then to Harvard, and became the First Lady of the United States. So, again, everything in her circumstances would've told her she was limited, but she had parents who pushed her, she had people in her community who saw something good in her, and so it absolutely propelled her to greatness.

Arianna Huffington, a Greek immigrant, marries a congressman, has two little girls, she's a stay-at-home congressman's wife, and her husband cheats on her. And it's public. She was humiliated by this. But Arianna Huffington turned that around, of course, and became a talking head. Then she starts *Huffington Post* and it gets bought by AOL. And, well, the rest is history; she's a billionaire.

And so, these three very different women, very different upbringings in the South, the Midwest, and an immigrant to the United States—they end up being very successful women because they knew who they were internally. So their confidence came from a place within. It didn't matter what other people said or how they tried to limit them. Everything we need to win in life is already inside of us, and that's really that little voice that says, "You can be an artist. You can be an author. You can be a journalist. You can be a doctor, a lawyer, an engineer. You can be the PTA president. You can start the Moms Against Drunk Driving organization." Whatever it is that women do, it's usually inside of us.

WHAT GOES INTO MAKING A BRAND?

You build your brand on two levels: One is conscious, the other unconsciously. You have control over both, but the unconscious brand building takes the most effort to manage. Case in point: I once worked with a woman who was negative every time I met her. She had a list of grievances and aired them at every available opportunity. There came a time when her career within the organization became stagnant because she sucked the oxygen out of the room. I'm sure you know people like that, and you would probably make that same decision.

Now, think about how other people see you. Are you the person who sucks the oxygen out of the room? Or are you the one who adds life, ingenuity, passion, and purpose to every meeting? What is your personal brand communicating every time you enter or exit a room?

I like to say that your brand is not always the product you deliver, but your delivery of the product. If you're a good marketer or an expert widget maker, but every time you interact with someone, you do the "sigh of agony"—you know, that longwinded sigh where your shoulders slump—it doesn't matter how good your product is. If your delivery makes customers or clients uncomfortable, they won't be coming back anytime soon.

No one wants to work with constantly negative people or, on the flip side, those who are positive and fun to be with but who just sit around and don't get things done. People may like you, but will they hire you? Promote you? Buy from you? Engage you? Remember, not competence or confidence, but competence and confidence. That's the "click" we want to find for your brand.

One more way to look at your brand is to consider the kind of energy you put into it: Is your energy negative or positive? Are you a "glass half full" or "glass half empty" person? I'm not saying that you must be a "glass half full" type; we all have our natural inclinations. What I am saying is that you have to understand how your energy comes across. If you are always perceived as unfavorable, it's going to impact your brand. It's also vital to "filter" the water in your glass to be appropriate for the work environment. For the "glass half full" person, bad corporate news may be met with "Oh well, tomorrow's another day," when a more serious tone is expected, and vice versa. The good news, generally speaking, is that you can learn how to temper your natural inclinations and build on your executive presence so that your brand and your delivery are focused and effective.

STEPS FOR BUILDING A STRONG BRAND

To build a good brand for yourself, you first must define what "good" means to you. What, exactly, do you want to portray? Frankly, there is no right or wrong answer. I think everyone's definition of what makes a "good brand" is slightly different. It also depends on the organization. Some companies hire for a specific type of brand and actively encourage it throughout the employment process.

So it becomes a delicate balance of how you want to show up and what it will take to be effective and, honestly, rewarded within the organization. Ultimately, you must be true to yourself and build a brand with which you can be comfortable.

But more broadly, you want to think of your brand as the legacy you want to leave. Once you leave the physical world, how do you want others to think of you and what do you want them to say? That is your legacy. I find that when I ask this question in my branding workshops it cuts deeper and differently. We tend to me more guarded and hypersensitive to our legacy because this reflects what people think about us in our totality, not just associated with a moment in time, our job, education, but our souls, the core of who we are what we contributed to the world and what imprint we left behind.

That said, here are some general rules for positive brand building:

Start from strength. How you show up at the beginning matters. Make a good first impression and your brand will come built-in. Looking someone in the eye, having a firm handshake, and how you are carrying yourself all help create and communicate a strong brand. Conversely, the same holds true for when you make a poor impression. That can linger as well. Be attuned to how you show up. Take a moment to be composed, quiet the fears, and know and feel you are accomplished. I often tell my clients "you only have one time to make a first impression, so why not make it positive and memorable?

Don't sacrifice your principles. You must lead with courage, conviction, and compassion. If you're in a position of authority in your career, this is not just important: it's imperative. On courageous leadership, the person who can tell the truth, who has the courage of conviction that this is the right thing to do, and also has compassion for the team and the company is the one who will stand out and be looked at as a leader. Know what you stand for and be true to your principles.

Guard your brand. This means social media and media in general. If you are going to be quoted in a story, understand the context and intent of the story. Don't mix business with pleasure on social media. When you are vacationing you are in a different mindset than in your professional world. Don't allow the two to collide if it's not flattering to your brand or business. In fact, don't allow others to capture certain photos. With such interconnnectivity between our work and personal lives we can become a bit too comfortable and overshare.

People may never tell you about your distasteful or risque photos but it will cause damage to your career and brand. According to Business News Daily, 75 percent of hiring professionals believe that checking a candidate's or employee's social media profile is an acceptable way to vet them (Cotriss, 2022). This will only increase as social media platforms continue to expand.

BEING A CHANGE AGENT

We often feel like we have to wait for change to happen, but true leaders act as change agents, forcing change upon a situation, team, or workplace when it's needed the most. Change agents are important because they make things happen in an organization, often powerful and influential leaders. As we will see in this chapter, they can do this by forcing change, "editing" change, or contributing to it.

HOW DO YOU DEAL WITH CHANGE?

Not everyone responds to change in the same way. In fact, in your evolution as a leader, you have probably noticed various types of people in the organizations where you've worked.

There are people who only like the change they have created. These people like to "put glitter on something" by just tweaking and adding ideas, they resist change unless it has value they can see, touch, and feel. It's important to remember that those different types of people all work in the same company, often on the same team. They won't react to change the same way you do or even the same way other team members and employees do. The truth is, organizations are changing—evolving, growing, adapting—all the time. So understanding how you deal with change is important.

Case in point: Recently, I worked with a leadership team. When we administered the CliftonStrenghts assessment to identify your unique talent DNA that explains how your naturally think, feel and behave. 95 percent of the team showed empathy as one of their bottom five strengths. This spoke volumes in terms of why the team weren't connecting with their customers or each other. Not only did members of this group want to know why they weren't being successful and meeting their sales targets they needed to know how to make a shift.

We had to embark on both a change and leadership initiative. The two team members where empathy were in their top five were women. This allowed them an elevated validation in the group because they were able to team up with senior members on the team that managed the large accounts and provide them advice and strategies on how to connnect with their current and prospective customers. They were reluctant to take on the challenge but with reassurance and encouragement they excelled with their new responsibilities, whereas prior they were going unnoticed with their talents being mocked instead of celebrated.

Discussions around how you feel about change are important because you can't be successful as a change agent if you don't recognize how you feel about the change in the first place.

HOW DO YOU FEEL ABOUT CHANGE?

Let's stop for a minute and focus on you. How do you feel about change? Answer a few simple questions to understand your feelings about change a little better:

How does change make you feel? When the idea of change arises, do you get uncomfortable or optimistic? The only appropriate way to respond to change is to embrace it, but first, you must understand how it makes you feel to ensure that you can respond appropriately.

Do you prefer to force change or be along for the ride? Some people like to be the change instigator, while others prefer to be the change "editor." By that, I mean that they excel at taking someone else's idea and applying their strengths, skillset, and expertise to making it even better.

Do you like to brainstorm about change alone or in a group? Some people are more comfortable working in a vacuum as often as they can. Others excel in a group atmosphere where they can bounce ideas off one another.

Do you fear change? Finally, many of us shrink from change because we know it will upset our personal and professional applecart.

Knowing how you react to change will help you be clear, focused, and empathetic as you begin to recognize that other groups of people have different needs—and you begin to address what those needs are when it comes to change.

THE TAKEAWAY

Change is vital for success, not only your success as a current or future leader, but the success of your team, your department, and, ultimately, your entire organization as well. To be a change agent, you must recognize both the power and pace of change. It doesn't happen overnight, nor do people always respond well to change. How you deal with change is also about fueling your mind with positive energy so you are equipped and prepared to manage the uncertainties associated with change (Gordon, 2007). And then, if you know your stuff, know you deserve a seat at that table."

Understanding the power of change and learning to be comfortable with it helps "brand" you as a change agent, something every company needs in these sophisticated, complicated times.

Why does this matter so much? Simple: Leaders want to see that you are on board to go to the next level. Being a change agent is about connecting the dots for other people as well as yourself.

TAKING CONTROL OF YOUR CAREER

Nothing requires more resilience than navigating a career that can span decades—and must weather the storm of countless setbacks, obstacles, challenges, and outright roadblocks. This chapter looks at the long term and provides sound strategies for creating habits that, if begun now, can ensure smooth sailing as you navigate your career and your journey from competence to confidence.

PLANNING FOR POTENTIAL

I think that very often, women don't necessarily plan their careers. We have a penchant for feeling lucky if we get a job, let alone a promotion, and "wing it" from opportunity to opportunity until we find ourselves in some position that wasn't necessarily achieved by some grand design.

Case in point: I recently talked to a client who wanted to be the Chief HR officer for her company. Rather than just want it, she had actually studied the career trajectories, duties, and success habits of other CHROs to become clear on what she'd need to be successful in that role. I was impressed by her "background investigation" into her dream job and immediately thought that this person would get there because she had her career road map carefully and thoroughly planned.

On the other hand, my transition into HR was by default. I began my career in the HR industry because of the paranoia surrounding Y2K. There was a shortage of IT programmers and technical recruiters to intenivize then leave organizations to join others. I knew nothing about IT, STEM or coding but I spent tireless hours researching and being prepared for my first interview. Because there was some concern that I wasn't a professional recruiter I began my career as a technical staffing coordinator, where I was the first point of contact with the programmers. After performing in that role for three months I was promoted to a technical recruiter. My promotion was a combination of the programmers wanting to continue with me as their representative versus starting over with anyone else. I continued to develop and build my career in HR to where I am today.

I always envisioned being the CEO of an organization but as Ursula Banks stated, HR is not the functional track that leads to a CEO position in a large organization. So I built my own road to becoming a CEO at my own firm, Reimagine OD. I built a network, worked diligently, and positioned myself as I moved into the space I currently occupy helping organizations, women of color and women excel to consistent and sustainable greatness.

That said, I challenge future leaders to know what their long-term plans are. Notice I said "their" long-term plans, not the plans that their team or friends, or family, or spouses think are appropriate. Know yourself, know your goals, know your desires and passions, and make that the target of your goals and plans moving forward. It doesn't have to be the "top". It's okay to say you want to be a VP or senior VP instead of the CEO of a large corporation. Whatever the ultimate goal, know what will be expected of you in that position. Just like my client, who thoroughly researched the job description and unwritten expectations of being head of HR, know the ins and outs of what you're shooting for to make sure that you're fully equipped once your goal is met.

THE ART OF SIDE HUSTLES AND DUALPRENEURSHIP

Why everyone should have a side hustle. When most of us think of a side hustle or hear the term side hustle, we immediately think another job, a second job, something else that we have add to our plate to earn money or another task that is going to take us away from our family. But I have a much different perspective on side hustle.

When I think of side hustle, I think of opportunity, and not just opportunity for financial income but an opportunity to build your confidence, a sense of freedom and accomplishment. It gives you an opportunity for your creative prowess to come out. It gives you an opportunity to be competitive in an ever-changing economic world, to have something else that simply belongs to you that you can have as a backup plan. It also allows you an opportunity to tap into or back into a passion that you care about, or maybe you let go of years ago for whatever reason. Once again, it's something that's uniquely yours.

Now, I mention income in the side hustle conversation last because although I do believe side hustles can absolutely and should eventually bring about financial rewards, the additional income is the byproduct of pouring your passion into something that you enjoy. Additional income will come once you have perfected what your side hustle is.

And it brings so much more to you, to your life, to your identity, and to your brand than solely the income.

Once again, the side hustle philosophy is so important. I think it gives you an opportunity to build something that's uniquely yours. And let's take a great example. Let's say you had aspired in your past to be a journalist. Your career did not go in that direction for whatever reason, but you still enjoy writing, you still enjoy reading, you still enjoy research. Now you can, say, write for a digital magazine. Starting out, they may not pay you, but once you have so many readers and such a following, it might manifest itself into being another financial stream of income for you. And this is what I mean in terms of pouring into your passion, and then realizing and figuring itself out in a way that becomes a financial income and outlet for you. And we all have had many things in our lives where we gave it up for whatever reason, and our career took off in a different direction, but we still have these nuggets, whether it's crafts or whether it's entertainment, comedy, acting, whatever it is, we've all left remnants of ourselves behind. How do you pick those up and turn them into a side hustle, to be able to be creative, tap into your passion, have something that's uniquely yours that eventually can manifest and turn itself into a financial outcome for you? And this is why it's important for everyone to have a side hustle, because once again, it gives you something to fall back on as well if you're in that position, if you're with that organization, if you're working with a manager that's not feeding into your purpose, feeding into your progression, you're being looked over time and time again for promotion, you're being disenfranchised. How do you have something where you can say, "Okay, I can walk away from this and do something else that I've already laid some of the foundation for"?

And really, that's the essence of having that side hustle.

FIVE STEPS FOR SETTING QUALITY CAREER GOALS

Setting goals is one thing, but reaching them is another. To ensure that you are sufficiently prepared to navigate the career success you want, here are five steps for setting quality career goals:

1. **Have a strategy,** not just a plan. The more strategically you can plan, the more proficiently you can prepare. For instance, today's companies want their leaders to have more global experience. Knowing this ahead of time, you can tailor your activities, opportunities, and credentials by casting a wider net and taking any and all international opportunities that arise in your current and future positions. Barring those, you can seek mentorship opportunities or take classes or seminars to increase the amount of globalization in your professional portfolio.
2. **Keep learning**—stay curious. Knowing your "dream job" requirements, you can better ascertain if you have the right credentials to get it. Ask yourself: "Do I have the right degree, training, and experience for what I want to do?" If not, what should you do? Take training and courses to get the skills you'll need? Figure this out ahead of time, and your goals will be easier to obtain.
3. **Invest in yourself.** As I suggested in the previous tip, sometimes you need to be willing to invest in yourself in the form of classwork, training, magazine and web subscriptions, books and seminars, online learning, etc. (You may also need to invest in appropriate business attire.) All this may involve you asking for development, training, and even certification in certain courses and taking advantage of a tuition reimbursement plan if your

employer offers one. If not, pace yourself and make the financial investment on your own.

4. **Chart your progress.** Be sure to measure your progress so that you know where you are on your career trajectory. When we have a plan in place, it's critical to measure and reassess to ensure our current goals are met continually. You may be ahead of your timeline or behind it. You may have achieved certain goals and forgotten to mark or measure them. By continually "checking in" to mark your progress, you can assess where you've been, where you are ... and where you need to be.
5. **Bounce!** We learned in an earlier chapter how to bounce when challenges, setbacks, or obstacles litter our path. On that note, don't be afraid to change course, even midstream, if the right opportunity presents itself. Leadership changes, our priorities change, teams dissolve, or members are reassigned, and we often find ourselves at a point far afield from where we thought we wanted to be. You may learn more about the role you thought you wanted and realize, halfway there, that what you want is just a little bit closer to another place or direction. That's fine. We call that growth, evolution, and progress, and it's what resilience—and this chapter—is all about.

In addition to those five steps, here is an important thing to remember about navigating your career: Time will pass whether or not you do anything about your career.

There is a great story of a woman who graduated from law school when she was eighty-five. After her story appeared in the press, people came up and said to her, "Oh my God, who is going to hire you at eighty-five?" She replied that it did not matter because she would be eighty-five anyway, but now she had a law degree.

The truth is that time passes. Yesterday has passed, today will pass, and, if we're lucky, tomorrow will pass, too. What matters is how you use that time strategically to make or break you as a leader.

We must be conscious of the passing of time and use it, thoughtfully, to our advantage. Too many of us take time for granted. We never move forward, only side-to-side—or even backward. If you let life push you around with no action plan for moving forward in a strategic, thoughtful, or purposeful way, you'll never get to your desired destination.

I have observed from women over forty that, suddenly, they begin to wonder how they got where they are. I often hear them say, "This is not the life I had planned for myself." But I wonder: Did they have any plan at all? I tend to think that we are not as intentional about our lives and where we are going as we think we are or ought to be. And so this is an invitation to create that intention—a place to create a road map for your life.

THE TAKEAWAY

Remember, it's your journey from competence to confidence. It's your career. Your career is your responsibility, not your company's and not anyone else's. It's important to concentrate your energy on what you want and not what anybody else can provide for you.

We control our careers by setting goals, focusing on a particular direction, taking feedback, and being open to that feedback. Charting and changing your course means that you may need to shift some of your behaviors and be willing to learn new ways of doing things you thought you had already covered.

Navigating your career from competence to confidence is as much about changing directions as it is about following a straight, linear path. Being willing to develop yourself as your company progresses sends a strong signal about your leadership potential. Just because your company won't pay to develop you doesn't mean that you shouldn't take a course here or there anyway. Take accountability for yourself and your actions!

Investing in yourself doesn't have to break the bank. For just $25, you can attend a professional association meeting where you'll get to hear a great speaker who may actively change your life. I am so inspired by others that I never miss an opportunity to hear someone new speak because I know that, at the very least, I'm going to hear a new perspective on some aspect of my career that I might be taking for granted.

I could go on, but the point here is this: You are the CEO of your career, and the kinds of things that we do in terms of preparing ourselves for that make all the difference, not only in how we lead but for which organization. My belief is: "if you aren't willing to invest in yourself for your development why would you expect anyone to sacrifice finances to invest in you?

SUCCESS AND LIKEABILITY

Okay, so all a woman has to do is ignore society's expectations, be ambitious, sit at the table, work hard, and then it's smooth sailing all the way. What could go wrong?

In 2003, Columbia Business School professor Frank Flynn and New York University professor Cameron Anderson experimented with testing perceptions of men and women in the workplace.1 They started with a Harvard Business School case study about a real-life entrepreneur named Heidi Roizen. The case described how Roizen became a successful venture capitalist by using her "outgoing personality ... and vast personal and professional network [that] included many of the most powerful business leaders in the technology sector." Flynn and Anderson assigned half of the students to read Heidi's story and gave the other half the same level with just one difference—they changed the name "Heidi" to "Howard."

Professors Flynn and Anderson then polled the students about their impressions of Heidi or Howard. The students rated Heidi and Howard as equally competent, making sense since "their" accomplishments were completely identical. Yet while students respected both Heidi and Howard, Howard came across as a more appealing colleague. On the other hand, Heidi was seen as selfish and not "the type of person you would want to hire or work for." The same data with a single difference—gender—created vastly different impressions.

This experiment supports what research has already clearly shown: success and likeability are positively correlated for men and negatively correlated for women. When a man is successful, he is liked by both men and women. When a woman is successful, people of both genders like her less. This truth is both shocking and unsurprising: shocking because no one would ever admit to stereotyping based on gender and unsurprising because clearly, we do.

Decades of social science studies have confirmed what the Heidi/Howard case study so blatantly demonstrates: we evaluate people based on stereotypes (gender, race, nationality, and age, among others). Our stereotype of men holds that they are providers, decisive, and driven. Our stereotype of women holds that they are caregivers, sensitive, and communal. Because we characterize men and women in opposition to each other, professional achievement and all the traits associated with it get placed in the male column. By focusing on her career and taking a calculated approach to amassing power, Heidi violated our stereotypical expectations of women. Yet by behaving in the same manner, Howard lived up to our stereotypical expectations of men. The result? I liked him, I disliked her.

I believe this bias is at the very core of why women are held back. It is also at the very core of why women hold themselves back. For men, professional success comes with positive reinforcement at every step of the way. For women, even when they're recognized for their achievements, they're often regarded unfavorably. Journalist Shankar Vedantam once catalogued the derogatory descriptions of some of the first female world leaders. "England's Margaret Thatcher," he wrote, "was called 'Attila the Hen.' Golda Meir, Israel's first female Prime Minister, was 'the only man in the Cabinet.' President Richard Nixon called Indira Gandhi, India's first female Prime Minister, 'the old witch.' And Angela Merkel, the current chancellor of Germany, has been dubbed 'the iron frau.'"

I have seen this dynamic play out over and over. When a woman excels at her job, both male and female coworkers will remark that she may be accomplishing a lot but is "not as well-liked by her peers." She is probably also "too aggressive", "not a team player", "a bit political", "can't be trusted", or "difficult." These are some common statements said about many women in senior-level positions. Yet, the world seems to be asking why we can't be less like Heidi and more like Howard.

Most women have never heard of the Heidi/Howard study. Most of us are never told about this downside of achievement. Still, we sense this punishment for success. We're aware that when a woman acts forcefully or competitively, she's deviating from expected behavior. If a woman pushes to get the job done, if she's highly competent, she's acting like a man if she focuses on results rather than pleasing others. And if she exhibits too many male-associated qualities, some will dislike her.

THE MYTH OF DOING IT ALL

HAVING IT ALL. Perhaps the greatest trap ever set for women was the coining of this phrase. Bandied about in speeches, headlines, and articles, these three little words are intended to be aspirational but instead make all of us feel like we have fallen short. I have never met a woman, or man, who has stated emphatically, "Yes, I have it all." Because no matter what any of us has—and how grateful we are for what we have, no one has it all.

Nor can we. The very concept of having it all flies in the face of the basic laws of economics and common sense. As Sharon Poczter, professor of economics at Cornell, explains, "The antiquated rhetoric of 'having it all' disregards the basis of every economic relationship: the idea of trade-offs. All of us are dealing with the constrained optimization that is life, attempting to maximize our utility based on parameters like career, kids, relationships, etc., doing our best to allocate the resource of time. Due to the scarcity of this resource, therefore, none of us can 'have it all,' and those who claim to are most likely lying."

"Having it all" is best regarded as a myth. And like many myths, it can deliver a helpful cautionary message. Think of Icarus, who soared to great heights with his man-made wings. His father warned him not to fly too near the sun, but Icarus ignored the advice. He soared even higher, his wings melted, and he crashed into the sea. Pursuing both a professional and personal life is a noble and attainable goal, up to a point. Women should learn from Icarus to aim for the sky, but keep in mind that we all have real limits.

Instead of pondering the question "Can we have it all?," we should be asking the more practical question "Can we do it all?" And again, the answer is no. Each of us makes choices constantly between work and family, exercising and relaxing, making time for others and taking time for ourselves. Being a parent means making adjustments, compromises, and sacrifices every day. For most people, sacrifices and hardships are not a choice, but a necessity. About 65 percent of married-couple families with children in the United States have two parents in the workforce, with almost all relying on both incomes to support their household. Being a single working parent can be even more difficult. About 30 percent of families with children are led by a single parent, with 85 percent of those led by a woman.

Mothers who work outside the home are constantly reminded of these challenges. Tina Fey noted that when she was promoting the movie *Date Night* with Steve Carell, a father of two and star of his own sitcom, reporters would grill Fey on how she balances her life, but never posed that question to her male costar. As she wrote in *Bossypants*, "What is the rudest question you can ask a woman? 'How old are you?' 'What do you weigh? No, the worst question is 'How do you juggle it all?' ... People constantly ask me, with an accusatory look in their eyes."

Fey nails it. Employed mothers and fathers both struggle with multiple responsibilities, but mothers also have to endure the rude questions and accusatory looks that remind us that we're shortchanging both our jobs and our children. As if we needed reminding. Most women do a great job worrying about what's not done and if they measure up. We compare our efforts at work to those of our colleagues, usually men, who typically have far fewer responsibilities at home. Then we compare our efforts at home to those mothers who dedicate themselves solely to their families. Outside observers reminding us that we must be struggling—and failing—is just bitter icing on an already soggy cake.

Trying to do it all and expecting that it all can be done exactly right is a recipe for disappointment. Perfection is the enemy. Gloria Steinem said it best: "You can't do it all. No one can have two full-time jobs, have perfect children and cook three meals ... Superwoman is the adversary of the women's movement."

Dr. Laurie Glimcher, dean of Weill Cornell Medical College, said the key for her in pursuing her career while raising children was learning where to focus her attention. "I had to decide what mattered and what didn't and I learned to be a perfectionist in only the things that mattered." In her case, she concluded that scientific data had to be perfect, but reviews and other mundane administrative tasks could be considered good enough at 95 percent. Dr. Glimcher also said she made it a priority to get home at a reasonable hour, adding that when she got there, she refused to worry about whether "the linens were folded or the closets were tidy. You can't be obsessive about these things that don't matter."

It is impossible to control all the variables when it comes to parenting.

HOW WOMEN LEAD DIFFERENTLY

Female Leaders tend to be more interactive, wanting to keep interactions extended and vital until the interaction has worked through its emotional content.

Tend more toward participative in teams—to find ways in which colleagues are complementary. It is probable that higher oxytocin levels affect this leadership quality—the more support women build around them, the lower their stress level, and the more effective they may be as leaders.

Tend to collaborate connectively by seeking possible connections between each person's different ideas—and try to find developmental elements in the connectivity.

Tend to enjoy solving problems with others, for many of the brain-related reasons described above.

Tend to be more inductive in leadership problem-solving than men. This is about listening, hearing viewpoints, building a sense of what to do in a woman's mind from hearing all voices around her. When she knows what to do, she's not as worried as a man might be about proving it with data: she can already see that it works.

Tend to define themselves by being relationally literate, keeping personal or workplace relationships intact. Women are reluctant to brag about their accomplishments.

Tend to feel the work should speak for itself and want to be recognized for the work without having to draw attention to it.

Provide as much hands-on connection to the coworker as possible. Given their higher oxytocin levels and greater verbal-emotive ability, women are more likely than men to try to ascertain the exact needs of a person, sensing how morale-needs impact productivity on a daily basis.

Emphasize complex and multitasking activities, actions, team development—expanding leadership into various tasks and away from dominance by one task. They discover a panoply of possibilities for a product, as well as within a worker's untapped capabilities. With a brain that cross talks between hemispheres constantly, women tend to value multiple connections.

Work constantly toward helping others (especially men) express emotions in words rather than just in actions. Greater verbal-emotive brain activity stimulates this (as well as the following attribute of female leaders).

Search for a method of direct empathy when someone's feelings are hurt ("How are you feeling? Tell me about it. What happened?"), even at the expense of other current goals.

Relinquish personal, daily independence in order to be cognizant of other's needs. Female leaders are more likely than male leaders to adapt their schedule toward concentration on a person's immediate needs; their higher oxytocin and more active cingulate gyrus help them to be more attuned to the specific needs of many individuals at a time.

Promote the development of skills and talents in coworkers through an emphasis on verbal encouragement and praise. Females' higher oxytocin and reliance on verbal encouragement often lead them to issue lots of praise, not realizing that many men are suspicious of too much praise.

Try to help the coworker resolve emotional conflicts and stresses so that the whole bonding system can feel better. An individual's immediate sense of distress or anxiety triggers oxytocin in a woman, which can direct her to try to quickly defuse obvious conflicts, more so than her male counterpart.

HOW WOMEN MANAGE DIFFERENTLY

Female managers tend to be more descriptive in their management—they tend to describe what they are looking for, and spend more time detailing to employees—and hearing from employees—how to accomplish the goal.

Tend to feel their work life disrupted by direct conflict, so they tend to accomplish more behind the scenes conflicts. With higher oxytocin levels and lower testosterone levels (such as greater internal push toward continuity of relationship and less push toward disruption of relationship), and even though women will indeed say nasty things about each other, they will generally try to hide them so that at least a semblance of relationship still exists. Because women remember interactions, including conflicts, longer than men and men may perceive that women are holding onto a grudge, and thus distrust female managers.

HOW WOMEN LEAD MEETINGS DIFFERENTLY

Women tend to look around the room for more verbal opinions than men do. They also tend more than men to want data fleshed out with "the human factor."

Tend to let people speak longer to make their point than male leaders do.

Tend to ask others what direction they want to go in, and they accept more oblique references to how a process might be furthered. This can be seen as a lack of confidence instead of simply a gender difference.

Tend to have longer memories for conflicts, emotional battles, and emotional stresses from the last meeting than men do. Women are more likely to remember specific situations, the relational details about looks or tones of voice, or competitive maneuverings than men.

PERCEPTIONS OF AMBITION

For some reason, ambition has become a dirty word. It's dirty to those who want to stifle you, extinguish your dreams, keep you in a box and limit your imagination. To those who foster growth, development and design thinking, ambition is a positive. Upon saying I was ambitious to a C-Suite level leader in my past, I was told to never say that because to others in the company it meant that you weren't happy where you were, you were always on the quest for something else and it would appear as if you were never satisfied. I knew in that moment I wouldn't continue to have a flourishing career if I remained there if that was truly the mentality of the leadership team. From my perspective, you should always look to improve. I have a saying, that if you can't add something new to your resume annually, you are not in a growth environment. I thrive on growth and challenges, and for me, not being ambitious is an undesirable mindset.

Women believe it is essential to have ambitions or a strong desire to achieve success in life. The importance of ambition to women is generally quite high, with 59 percent overall who believe it is essential to life and work. However, differences can be seen from country-to-country with the highest levels in India (89 percent, very important), followed by Mexico (82 percent) and the U.S. (68 percent). The importance of having any ambitions in life is significantly lower in France (41 percent, critical) and Japan (28 percent).

Most women do not call themselves "ambitious," and they are divided about whether being described as "ambitious" in the workplace is positive. The majority of women consider themselves to be ambitious. However, only three-in-ten (31 percent) women overall say they are proud to call themselves ambitious. More feel that they are ambitious but wouldn't describe themselves this way publicly (34 percent). One-quarter (26 percent) say they pursue opportunities but are unsure about calling themselves ambitious.

While in the workplace, more women believe it is very positive to be described as motivated (56 percent) or confident (48 percent) than ambitious (40 percent). And, likeability (53 percent) is significantly more positive than assertiveness (36 percent) or competitiveness (30 percent).

Women in India (69 percent), the U.S. (51 percent), and Germany (46 percent) were most likely to view being called ambitious as very positive, compared to other markets.

REINVENTION REFLECTION

To continue this discussion about ambition with my leader, my look of confusion caused her to explain further. However, on this one day she told me that it was a career derailer to tell individuals in the organization that I was ambitious. She said, leaders, who were men, largely thought of the word ambitious as negative. My look of confusion caused her to explain further that ambition means you are not happy where you are but that you are looking to go elsewhere and that is viewed negatively by leadership. I immediately retorted with; well, I am looking to move on in my career. I will never be satisfied simply sitting in my current role without a plan for moving forward, I feel with my work, dedication to the organization and knowledge should afford me the right to say that I am ambitious and purporting any other perspective would be disingenuous. I knew in that moment that it wasn't the place for me and that she wasn't willing to be an advocate or ally for my continued advancement. Therefore, I executed Step 5 from our "Taking Control of Your Career" chapter and bounced. Conversely, I have observed many women that have been at a comparable level in their organizations for over a decade with no plan in place for advancement despite wanting to advance.

PUTTING PERSONAL AMBITIONS ABOVE PROFESSIONAL

When considering different career and personal life ambitions, the survey results showed that external manifestations of ambition (career, wealth, skills) rank at the bottom of the list of importance. Almost universally, personal goals (health, parenting, and relationships) ranked much higher in defining ambition.

Being as healthy as possible tops the list, rated very important by two-thirds of the women surveyed overall (65 percent), while acquiring wealth, a traditional outcome of ambition, is at the bottom of the list, with only 30 percent rating it as very important. Notable findings by market include:

According to TribuneIndia (2021), 88 percent of women surveyed in India want to improve their skills and abilities to become more employable as compared with 97 percent in Brazil and 90 percent in Mexico

I understand that, regardless of how hard I work, the problems I am solving for women and people of color will never be completely solved in my lifetime. But what drives me is knowing I am making the path smoother for current and future generations. Perhaps they will have opportunities to work in environments devoid of gender, race, sexual orientation, religious, ability and ethnicity biases. I am content with my legacy, centering on "a leader who fought the good fight to foster equity and equality for all."

Where do you personally think ambition comes from, is it solely 'project' based, as in a person will feel the most ambitious when they have found the career that suits them best/when they have a family/a hobby or extra-curricular activity? And in that case, can you only be ambitious about one thing at a time?

Ambition is innate. It doesn't matter what job or career you have, ambition comes from within. I was just as ambitious as a telemarketer and encyclopedia sales representative, flight attendant and waitress as I am as a researcher, executive, professor, entrepreneur, and author. It is really who you are. You can see ambition in people when they perform their jobs. The barista who takes just a couple seconds more to ask about your day or how to spell your name correctly. The librarian who goes the extra mile to secure a book for you. The finance team member who explains the budgeting process when you look bewildered.

If you are innately ambitious, more than likely, you are focused on more than one thing, but you do have to monitor not becoming overwhelmed, burning out or allowing that ambition to counteract with the ability to get projects over the finish line.For those that might not have ambitious tendencies, I coach team members to focus on one project or goal at a time. Accomplishment fuels the thirst for wanting more and bigger accomplishments. There is no bigger confidence booster than completing a goal. It enhances your pride and boosts your confidence level.

LEADERSHIP SELF-ASSESSMENT: HOW EFFECTIVE ARE YOU?

Knowing yourself is critical to being an effective leader. Building self-awareness and understanding your tendencies and motivational drivers can enable you to unlock potential in yourself and your team. You can't lead others without understanding, reconciling with and knowing who you are. It's impossible. We have to know ourselves before we can lead and manage others.

"Self-awareness is about developing your capacity to sense how you're coming across, to have undistorted visibility into your own strengths and weaknesses, and to be able to gauge the emotions you're personally experiencing," says Harvard Business School Professor, Joshua Margolis, in the online course Leadership Principles. "If you're going to mobilize others to get things done, you can't let your own emotions get in the way."

According to an analysis by Korn/Ferry International, companies with higher rates of financial return tend to employ professionals with high degrees of self-awareness. Research also shows that self-aware leaders report having:

- Greater effectiveness in the workplace
- Better relationships with colleagues
- An improved ability to identify and manage their emotions
- Reduced stress

Reaping these rewards can be achieved through honest self-assessment. By examining the patterns that emerge in how you view yourself, and how others experience you, you can identify ways to learn and develop as a leader. If you want to maximize your career trajectory and improve how you guide and manage teams, here are four ways you can assess your leadership effectiveness.

HOW TO ASSESS YOUR LEADERSIP EFFECTIVENESS

1. Complete a Self-Assessment

Questionnaires can be useful for identifying your motivations and strengths. In the online course Leadership Principles, participants complete two self-assessments: behavioral IQ and EI assessments.

By taking these assessments, learners can recognize behavioral patterns and gain insight into how they manage themselves and their colleagues.

This self-awareness is critical to effective leadership because it develops emotional intelligence—an ability that's possessed by 90 percent of top performers in the workplace. Through looking inward and answering questions with honesty and candor, you learn how to better command your emotions, as well as others', and build a foundation for your leadership approach.

2. Observe Yourself

In addition to self-assessments, observing a video recording of yourself can be a valuable way to learn more about your leadership tendencies. Taking part in this kind of exercise can enable you to gauge how you present yourself and exhibit attributes of different leadership styles, such as authenticity, humility, and faith. Engaging in critical self-observation can also help you overcome the vulnerability that comes with putting yourself in front of others as a leader, providing you with the confidence needed to inspire and influence your team.

3. Ask for Feedback

Beyond self-reflection, turn to those you interact and collaborate with for feedback on your effectiveness. Unlike management, leadership is less about administering and organizing, and more about aligning and empowering employees to pursue organizational goals.

By turning to your colleagues for thoughts on how they experience your leadership style, you can identify discrepancies in how you perceive yourself and chart a plan for improvement.

Soliciting and heeding feedback also helps develop clear lines of communication with your team, which is essential for building trust and driving performance.

Assessments have helped me understand my leadership, behavioral and communication styles of my team members and myself which has been invaluable to overall team collaboration and cohesion.

4. Build and Maintain a Robust Network

Leadership is a skill that must be honed over time. As you progress throughout your career, it's vital to cultivate a robust network you can rely on for coaching, support, and guidance. According to Benedictine University Professors Sorensen and Yaeger inform their students that exhibiting constructive leadership behaviors will attract the right individuals to your network.

Through networking, you can build a powerful resource that exposes you to new opportunities and drives your personal growth and success.

WHAT ARE LEADERSHIP COMPETENCIES?

Leadership competencies are a specific combination of knowledge, skills, and abilities (KSA) that represent effective leadership within an organization (Hollenbeck, McCall & Silzer, 2006).

What we can deduct from this definition is that there isn't one unique set of leadership competencies that works across all industries and companies. In fact, different leadership positions within a single organization may require different sets of knowledge, skills, and abilities.

Therefore, a lot of organizations work with a leadership competency framework, a collection of competencies they have identified as key for success and that's relevant for their leaders and their organization. The development of these competencies is crucial for effective succession planning.

TYPES OF LEADERSHIP COMPETENCIES

There are, however, certain skills and competencies that are essential for every leader, regardless of the industry and company they are in. Being able to understand and spot these leadership competencies enables HR to make better-informed decisions when it comes to hiring, developing, and promoting leaders.

The Society for Human Resource Management (SHRM) distinguishes three competency categories, namely:

- Competencies for leading the organization
- Competencies for leading others
- Competencies for leading the self

Other categorizations are possible too. Deloitte, for instance, talks about developable capabilities—learned factors that change over time and reflect what a leader can do, and leadership potential—innate factors which are hard(er) to develop, stable over time, and reflect how a person is.

In this article, we'll stick with the categories presented by SHRM. Please note that the below list of leadership competencies isn't exhaustive and that one competency can fit in more than one category.

Competencies for leading the organization:

1. Social Intelligence (SI)

According to Psychology Today, social intelligence is one of the best predictors of effective leadership and therefore one of the top leadership competencies. Social intelligence is about our capacity to understand different social situations and dynamics. It also comprises our ability to operate effectively in these various social situations.

2. Conflict management

This is a leadership competency that fits both this category as well as the 'competencies for leading others' category. It involves helping others in the organization, whether they are fellow leaders or people in your team, in avoiding or resolving interpersonal conflicts.

Conflict management is linked to something that organizational theorist, Fons Trompenaars, calls the reconciliation competency. Reconciliation is, as Trompenaars puts it, "the art of combining". Rather than making a choice between two seemingly opposite opinions, or asking people to compromise, you find a way to combine them.

3. Decision-making

Decision-making is one of the key leadership competencies because it's at the core of a leader's activities. A good leader knows when to make a decision by themselves, when to consult their team members or peers and get their opinion on a certain matter, and, perhaps most importantly, when to take a step back and let others decide.

4. Sharing a Compelling Vision

The company's vision—what your organization wants to be at some point in the future based on its goals and aspirations—is an important reason why people want to (continue to) work for you.

Leaders need to be able to share the company's vision in a compelling way. It should get both other people in the organization as well as candidates behind it.

5. Change Management

Organizations change constantly. Some of these changes are relatively small while others take place over a longer period of time. A good example of this are the automation and/or digitization processes many organizations are going through right now.

Effective leaders know how to prepare, support, and guide their people through these various organizational changes.

6. Interpersonal Skills

Interpersonal skills are also referred to as people skills or soft skills. Examples include, among others, active listening, giving and receiving feedback, (non) verbal communication, problem-solving skills, and teamwork.

7. Emotional Intelligence (EI)

Emotional intelligence is about our ability to understand people's emotions and emotional situations. It's also about our capacity to understand and manage our own emotions.

Emotional intelligence is made up of several components:

- Self-awareness – Knowing your strengths and weaknesses.
- Self-regulation – Being able to manage our own emotions.
- Motivation – People with high emotional intelligence usually also are highly motivated.
- Empathy – People with empathy and compassion tend to connect better with others.
- Social skills – The social skills of emotionally intelligent people show they genuinely care for and respect others.

8. Being a Good Coach & Being Trustworthy

Leaders need to be many different things to many different people. One of them is being a good coach, not just for those in their team but also for their peers.

This means, for example, knowing when to (gently) push someone to go outside their comfort zone, giving useful feedback when necessary, and helping people find their personal vision.

A word on trustworthiness is in order here, not just because trust is crucial for a successful coaching relationship. It's also vital for leaders in building and maintaining strong relationships with the people they manage.

Harvard Business School professor Frances Frei explains what the three component parts of trust are:

Being authentic – Put (very) simply this means be yourself, at all times.

Having rigor in your logic – This is about ensuring the quality of our logic and our ability to communicate it.

Empathy – Aiming our empathy directly towards the people we are interacting with, really listening to them and immersing ourselves in their perspectives.

9. Inclusiveness

Good leaders know how to create a work environment in which everybody feels welcome. They make sure that every employee is treated equally and respectfully, has the same opportunities and resources, and can participate and thrive. In other words: good leaders are inclusive.

According to research done by Harvard Business Review, inclusive leaders share the following 6 traits:

- A visible commitment – To diversity, challenge the status quo, hold others accountable, and make D&I a personal priority.
- Humility – They are modest about capabilities, admit mistakes, and create the space for others to contribute.
- Awareness of bias – They show awareness of personal blind spots, as well as flaws in the system, and work hard to ensure a meritocracy.
- Curiosity about others – They demonstrate an open mindset and deep curiosity about others, listen without judgment, and seek with empathy to understand those around them.
- Cultural intelligence – They are attentive to others' cultures and adapt as required.
- Effective collaboration – They empower others, pay attention to diversity of thinking and psychological safety, and focus on team cohesion.

10. People Management

When it comes to leading others, good people management is crucial. Depending on the leadership level, this involves the process of overseeing the training, development, motivation, and day to day management of employees.

Good leaders give their teams the five Cs of people management: clarity, context, consistency, courage, and commitment.

11. (Learning) Agility

If there's one thing we learned from 2020, it's how important it is to be able to quickly adapt to rapidly changing circumstances. This goes for everyone in the workforce, but especially for leaders as they need to support and guide others—and the organization— through these sometimes challenging times. As such, agile leaders aren't afraid of change; on the contrary, they embrace it.

Good leaders also have the ability to continually learn, unlearn, and relearn, also referred to as learning agility. They know how important it is to keep developing, growing, and using new strategies to tackle the increasingly complex problems they face in their organizations.

12. Industry Knowledge/Expertise

Yes, people change jobs, companies, and industries more often than they did ten years ago. And yes, developments in some areas go so rapidly that it might seem impossible to stay on top of them with everything else leaders have on their to-do lists.

Effective leaders, however, know that it's still essential to develop a certain expertise in the area and company they're leading in.

13. Managing Yourself

This goes for your workload, emotions, schedule, etc. If you're leading others, you need to be able to manage yourself—in the broadest sense of the term—first. Everyone has their own way of doing this, of course, but being well-organized, planning ahead, and prioritizing are key elements here.

14. Courage

Leaders often need to make decisions. Not every decision will be easy, and sometimes deciding to do something—or not—means taking a (big) risk. That requires courage. Courage also is about standing by your values and people and defending them in front of others when necessary.

15. Organizational Citizenship Behavior

Put simply, organizational citizenship behavior (OCB) is a term that's used to describe all the positive and constructive employee actions and behaviors that aren't part of their formal job description. It's anything that employees do, out of their own free will, that supports their colleagues and benefits the organization as a whole.

The five most common types of OCB are:

- Altruism: This occurs when an employee helps or assists another employee without expecting anything in return.
- Courtesy: This is polite and considerate behavior towards other people. Examples of courtesy at work include saying good morning, asking a co-worker how their holiday was, how their kids are doing, how a project they're currently working on is going, etc.
- Sportsmanship: This is about being able to deal with situations that don't go as planned and not demonstrating negative behavior when that happens.
- Conscientiousness: In a work setting, this means that employees don't just show up on time and stick to deadlines, but that they,

for instance, also plan ahead before they go on holiday so that their colleagues won't be drowning in a big workload.

- Civic virtue: This is about how employees support their company when they're not in an official capacity. Civic virtue can be demonstrated by employees signing up for business events such as fundraisers or running a (semi) marathon for a charity with a team of co-workers.

Empathy is the overarching leadership characteristic that compliments all of the previous leadership characteristics. Empathy is the capscity to shate and understand another's "state of mind" or emotion. To have the ability to put yourself in their "shoes". (cited from the Interational Journal of Caring Sciences 1 (3): 118-123 Authors: Ioannidou, F. & Konstantikaki, V.

Leaders need to set a good example to inspire others. One way of doing so is by demonstrating the OCB they would like to see in others themselves.

HOW TO DEVELOP LEADERSHIP COMPETENCIES

The short answer here is: by creating and implementing a leadership development plan. However, to explain that process properly, we would need to write another article (which we will be doing soon, so watch this space). In the meantime, here's a brief overview of how to develop some of the competencies listed above:

Leadership competencies for leading the organization: Peer mentoring and coaching can be a good option here, in combination with, for example, more formal training on topics such as conflict management and change management.

Leadership competencies for leading others: Here too, coaching can be very useful, especially for things like giving and receiving feedback, active listening, and (non) verbal communication. Depending on the leadership level, people management training is also important.

Leadership competencies for leading yourself: As for the industry/company expertise, leaders can learn a lot about the company, their product, and their people by themselves and from others within the organization. To improve their planning and time-management skills, they can follow a course and/or workshop.

Assessments have been fundamental to my growth and development. They have helped me understand that each and every trait, profile and characteristic has a positive and negative impact and perception. Without knowing this, one can feel either invincible or incompetent. However, assessments help you realize where your talents fit into various teams that align with your personal career goals.

I believe the philosopy and timing centered on executive coaching is entirely mismatched. In my observation, most professionals don't engage with an executive coach until they are well into their career at the director level and above. Women experience fewer opportunities for an executive coach and for Black women the opportunity is nearly non-existant. However, if we reflect on the benefits of having an executive coach one can easily see why those that are afforded this opportunity along with having exposure to internal (high potential) or leadership development programs careers accelerate at a faster pace.

BENEFITS OF AN EXECUTIVE COACH

- Helps you achieve your goals faster
- Provides accountability
- Identifies blind spots

- Fosters unbiased feedback
- Builds strategic visioning
- Helps you see yourself more clearly
- Learn new ways to respond
- Provide tools to help you leverage your existing strengths

7 SELF-ASSESSMENTS EVERY PROFESSIONAL WOMAN SHOULD TAKE

1. ClinftonStengths – analyzes what your natural strengths are; where you excel naturally versus being forced.
2. Everything DiSC by Wiley – provides insight into how you build and foster relationships, respond to conflict, how your solve problems and your naturual motivation
3. Hogan – provides leadership strengths, weaknesses, preferred work settings and reputation
4. E-IQ – measures the way you perceive and express yourself, develop and maintain relationships and cope with challenges
5. B-IQ – measures your specific behavioral style, the impact on others and how to prepare for better, forming positive relationships with those who have different behavioral styles and tendencies
6. IDI – Intercultural Development Inventory – measures your intercultural compentence and provides solutions for enhancing your cultural competence
7. Forte Communication Style Profile – identifies your natural communication style, preferences and stamina.

CONCLUSION

I hope that my readers are more BOLDER, CREATIVE, CONFIDENT and RESILIENT after reading this book. Too often, we allow circumstances, controlled and uncontrolled, to dictate our destiny. This is no longer the playground where we can play. Women have everything we need for success if we learn how to take the right tools from our toolbox for the job we want to achieve. No doubt, we still have a lot to overcome. Systemic oppression, the wage gap, glass ceilings, misogyny, and bias have been highlighted, but so many women have successfully navigated around these oppressive roadblocks, and you can too. We are doing it every day, but we must continue with a thoughtful, mentally balanced approach.

Women are undeniably powerful. As we continue to lean into our power and chant, "I am Unique, I am Amazing, I am Unstoppable."

My main reason for writing this book was to answer the question so many ask me daily; "How do you accomplish so much?" Hopefully, I was able to answer this question. I never say to anyone, "if I can do it, you can too." I think that is arrogant and dismissive. I *will* say, you can do whatever you want however you want to do it. My path may not be the most optimal path for you, but my goal is that we both arrive at the same destination, one where we feel fulfilled, respected, accomplished, appreciated, valued, and restored.

I am blessed beyond measure. I am living my dream every day by doing work that truly has purpose and has a positive impact on others. I want to continue working for the equity and equality of women and people of color in the workplace.

It would be amazing for me to look at any companies' website and see diversity disbursed amongst the executive leadership teams and Board of Directors. You know if it's at the Executive levels, it is representative throughout the organization.

For those seeking the entrepreneurial route, I want to see women's companies' sustainability increase at the 5-year mark and have access to more non-predatory funding so that women aren't investing all their personal finances. When your organization has adequate investment, you have business mentorship, financial modeling, and funds to bring on competitively-compensated team members for a real chance at growth and scalability.

I believe in the next 30 years, we can get there. I see some positive forward movement happening in 10 years, because laws are currently being put in place to address some of these issues. Representation and the wage gap have an opportunity for the largest turnaround.

I will continue amplifying these issues as I have throughout my life. We will remain diligent in chipping away at these issues by being resolute, determined, and insistent - until the iceberg cracks.

INSPIRATIONAL QUOTES OF LEADERS

These quotes are from great women with great insight into leadership; they are well experienced in a different specializations.

"The ability to learn is the most important quality a leader can have." – Padmasree Warrior (CEO & Founder, Fable).

"One of the criticisms I've faced over the years is that I'm not aggressive enough or assertive enough or maybe somehow, because I'm empathetic, it means I'm weak. I totally rebel against that. I refuse to believe that you cannot be both compassionate and strong." – Jacinda Ardern (Prime Minister of New Zealand)

"Do not follow where the path may lead. Go instead where there is no path and leave a trail." – Muriel Strode (Poet)

"Leadership is not a person or a position. It is a complex moral relationship between people based on trust, obligation, commitment, emotion, and a shared vision of the good." – Joanne Ciulla (Author and Educator)

"Our deepest fear is not that we are inadequate. Our deepest fear is that we are powerful beyond measure." – Marianne Williamson (Author and Activist)

"You are never too small to make a difference." – Greta Thunberg (Environmental Activist)

"If you're not making some notable mistakes along the way, you're certainly not taking enough business and career chances." – Sallie Krawcheck (CEO & Co-Founder, Ellevest)

"We need to accept that we don't always make the right decisions, that we'll screw up royally sometimes. Understand that failure is not the opposite of success; it's part of success." – Arianna Huffington (Founder & CEO, Thrive Global)

"Rarely are opportunities presented to you in a perfect way. In a nice little box with a yellow bow on top. 'Here, open it; it's perfect. You'll love it.' Opportunities – the good ones – are messy, confusing and hard to recognize. They're risky. They challenge you." – Susan Wojcicki (CEO, Youtube)

"Passion is energy. Feel the power that comes from focusing on what excites you." – Oprah Winfrey (Media Executive and Philanthropist)

"If you want to run for Prime Minister, you can. If you don't, that's wonderful, too. Shave your armpits, don't shave them. Wear flats one day, heels the next. These things are so irrelevant and surface to what it is all really about, and I wish people wouldn't get caught up in that. We want to empower women to do exactly what they want, to be true to themselves, to have the opportunities to develop." – Emma Watson (Actor and Activist)

"I learned always to take on things I'd never done before. Growth and comfort do not coexist." – Ginni Rometty (Executive Chairman, IBM)

"I always did something I was a little not ready to do. I think that's how you grow. When there's that moment of 'Wow, I'm not really sure I can do this,' and you push through those moments, that's when you have a breakthrough." – Marissa Mayer (CEO, Sunshine Products, formerly Lumi Labs, Inc.)

"Do what you feel in your heart to be right – for you'll be criticized anyway." – Eleanor Roosevelt (Former First Lady of the United States)

"Who you are surrounded by often determines who you become." – Vicky Saunders (Founder, SheEO)

"Magic happens when you connect people. I credit much of my success to always making it a point to truly get to know people and help them whenever I can. It's become the backbone of our firm's success. Women founders, in particular, are often highly skilled at making connections that can help advance their businesses." – Susan Macpherson (Founder & CEO, McPherson Strategies)

"Leadership is hard to define, and good leadership even harder. But if you can get people to follow you to the ends of the earth, you are a great leader." – Indra Nooyi (Former CEO, PepsiCo)

"Ninety percent of leadership is the ability to communicate something people want." – Dianne Feinstein (Senior United States Senator)

"Emotional intelligence is the ability to use emotion to increase your own and others' success." – Annie McKee (Author and Business Advisor)

"Leadership is about making others better as a result of your presence and making sure that impact lasts in your absence." – Sheryl Sandberg (COO, Facebook)

"It's OK to admit what you don't know. It's OK to ask for help. And it's more than OK to listen to the people you lead – in fact, it's essential." – Mary Barra (CEO, General Motors)

"Leadership should be more participative than directive, more enabling than performing." – Mary D. Poole (Author)

"With kids, they don't do what you want them to do when you want them to do it. Organizations don't necessarily, either. You've got to listen. You've got to learn how to influence." – Ellen J.

Kullman (President & CEO, Carbon)

"People respond well to those that are sure of what they want." – Anna Wintour (Editor-in-Chief, Vogue)

"Take criticism seriously, but not personally. If there is truth or merit in the criticism, try to learn from it. Otherwise, let it roll right off you." – Hillary Clinton (American Politician)

"Don't be intimidated by what you don't know. That can be your greatest strength and ensure that you do things differently from everyone else." – Sara Blakely (Founder & CEO, Spanx)

"Part of leadership is knowing when to go ahead with a decision that's within your authority because you're convinced it's the right thing, even if other people don't understand it at that point." – Dr. Ingrid Mattson (Professor, Huron University College)

"If you are committed to creating value and if you aren't afraid of hard times, obstacles become utterly unimportant. A nuisance perhaps, but with no real power. The world respects creation; people will get out of your way." – Candice Carpenter Olson (Co-CEO, Fullbridge)

"You have to look at your career and personal life at the big-picture level: it's a marathon, not a sprint. Doing that helps me feel OK during the weeks when one part of my life overwhelms the other." – Joanna Horsnail (Partner, Mayer Brown LLP)

"No one else is going to build the life you want for you. No one else will even be able to understand it completely. The most amazing souls will show up to cheer you along the way, but this is your game. Make a pact to be in it with yourself for the long haul, as your own supportive friend at every step along the way." – Tara Mohr (Leadership Coach and Author)

"I'm a maniacal perfectionist. And if I weren't, I wouldn't have this company." – Martha Stewart (Author and Television Personality)

"Success isn't about how much money you make; it's about the difference you make in people's lives." – Michelle Obama (Former First Lady of the United States)

"Define success on your own terms, achieve it by your own rules, and build a life you're proud to live." – Anne Sweeney (Former President, Disney ABC Television Group)

"Without being willing to fail and continually get back up again, I would never have been able to find the right market and establish my product within it." – Kelly Manthey (Group Chief Executive, Kin+Carta)

"A leader takes people where they want to go. A great leader takes people where they don't necessarily want to go but ought to be." – Rosalynn Carter (Former First Lady of the United States)

"I've always subscribed to the belief that the best leader is not one who has the most followers, but one who creates the most leaders.

I strive every day—and in every program and offers we have at Integrous Women—to create more conscious, confident, and soulful leaders who, in return, will build a better world for all." – Stephanie Courtillier (Founder, Integrous Women)

"The biggest risk of all is not taking one." – Mellody Hobson (President and co-CEO of Ariel Investments)

"You need to spend political capital – be unafraid to introduce people, compliment somebody when it's deserved and stand up for something you believe in, rather than just go with the flow." – Amy Schulman (Partner, Polaris Partners)

"Leadership is about the team—the culture they keep and embrace, it's about empathy for your customers, clients, employees and the communities where you do business, it's about doing the right thing for the right reasons, being confident enough to take risks and responsible enough to think of those who your decisions and risks may affect." – Kat Cole (COO & President of FOCUS Brands)

"Do not be afraid to make decisions. Do not be afraid to make mistakes." – Carly Fiorina (Former CEO, Hewlett-Packard)

"If one is lucky, a solitary fantasy can transform one million realities." – Maya Angelou (Civil Rights Activist and Poet)

"The size of your dreams must always exceed your current capacity to achieve them. If your dreams do not scare you, they are not big enough." – Ellen Johnson Sirleaf (Former President of Liberia)

"Making the decision not to follow a system or someone else's rules has allowed me to dig into what my strengths and gifts are without spending time feeling jaded or wasteful."– Ishita Gupta (Founder, Fear. less Magazine)

"Success is an exception, so be exceptional." – Malti Bhojwani (Professional Coach and Author)

"A good leader is able to paint a picture of a vision for the future and then enlist others to go on the journey with her. A truly conscious leader recognizes that it is not about her but that the team is looking for inspiration and direction. Keeping her ego in check is essential." – Tamra Ryan (CEO, Women's Bean Project)

"I have broken many glass ceilings—so I know it can be done." – Helen Clark (Former New Zealand Prime Minister and UNDP Administrator)

"You can and should set your own limits and clearly articulate them. This takes courage, but it is also liberating and empowering and often earns you new respect." – Rosalind Brewer (COO & Group President of Starbucks)

"I think it's a combination of personality traits that have helped me to succeed. Not only hard work– but patience, sacrifice and choosing my battles have all helped me to reach the point in my career to which I aspired, in a company I admired." – Katelyn Gleason (CEO & Founder of Eligible)

"Cultivate a network of trusted mentors and colleagues. Other people can give us the best insight into ourselves– and our own limitations. We must have the courage to ask for help and to request feedback to expand our vision of what's possible." – Maria Castañón Moats (Assurance Partner, PwC)

"Continuous learning leads to continuous improvement. Commit yourself to advancing your knowledge, skills, and expertise. The business environment is quickly changing, and your understanding of the leading practices, thinking, and emerging tools will help you manage for better results. Be a lifelong student." – Pamela Gill Alabaster (Chief Marketing & Communications Officer, Centric Brands)

"A woman is like a tea bag; you never know how strong it is until it's in hot water." – Eleanor Roosevelt

"Begin somewhere. You cannot build a reputation for what you intend to do." – Liz Smith, journalist

"What I have learned is that I don't take 'no' as a definite 'no'. I take it as a sign that you're either not the right person or it's not the right time." – Monique Rodriguez (Mielle Organics)

REFERENCES

- Beaman, L.; Duflo, E.; Pande, R.; & Top,1lova, P. (2012). Female leadership raises aspirations and educational attainment for girls: A policy experiment in India. Srin11f, 135(6068), 582-586. DOI:l0.1126/science .1212382
- Borkowski, S. C. & Ugras, Y.]. (1998). Business students and ethics: A meta-analysis . .fm1111al of /J11.1i11f.\.1 /;thin, 17, I II 7-1127. DOI:I0.1023/ A:I005748725174
- Boulouta, I. (2012). Hidden connections: The link between board gender diversity and corporate social performance. .frn-mwl of /J11.\i11f.\\ Dhirs, I I 3(2), 185-197. DOI: 10.1007 / sl055 !-012-1293-7
- Carli, L. and A. Eagly. 2011. Gender and leadership. In A. Bryman, D. Collinson, K. Grint, B.Jackson, and M. Uhl Bien, (Eds.), 17, SaJ<r I /tl11dhwk of /.nulmhi/J, 269-85. London: Sage Publications.
- C.ohen, P. N. & Huffman, M. L. (2007). Working for the woman? Female managers and the gender wage gap. A mniran .~rKiologiu1l /1n1in11, 72, 681-704. DOI: 10.1177 /000312240707200502

- Davison, H.K. & Burke, M.J. (2000). Sex discrimination in simulated employment contexts: A meta-analytic investigation. .fmmwl of\l1mlio11al JM1m•im; 56(2), 225-248. DOI: 10. I 006/jvbe.1999.1711
- Eagly, A. H. & Carli, L. L. (2007). '/11m11J<h /hr !t1l')•1i11lh: '/Jir tmlh r//Km/ how 11•1111r11 lwm1M /nulm. Boston, MA: Harvard Business School Press.
- Eagly, A.H.; Gartzia, L.; & Carli, L. L. (2014). Female advantage: Revisited. In S. Kumra, R. Simpson, & R.]. Burke (Eds.), '/Jir Oxj;11d ht1mll••1k of;:nuln iu 01w111iu1/irm• (pp. 153-174). New York, NY: Oxford Unh•ersity Press.
- Eagly, A.H. & Karau, S.J. (2002). Role congruity theo1y of prejudice toward female leaders. l\1•1hologiml/1n1in11, /09(3), 573-598. doi:I0.1037 /0033-295X.109.3.573
- Eagly, A.H.; Karau, S.J.; & Makhijani, M. G. (1995). Gender and the effectiveness ofleaders: A meta-analysis. I'<Jrlwlogim/ /J11/Min, 117, 125-145.
- Franke, G. R.; Crown, D. F.; & Spake, D. F. (1997). Gender differences in ethical perceptions of business practices: A social role theory perspective . .fo1111111/ ofli/J/1/in/ l"Jdwloizy, 82, 920-934. doi: 10.1037I/0021-9010.82.6.920
- Goldberg, P.A. (1968). Are women prejudiced against women? 1i1111.1adio11, 5(5), 28-30.
- Heilman, M. (2001). Description and prescription: How gender stereotypes prevent women's ascent up the organizational ladder . .f1111rnfll 11f S1N:ifll ls.mPs, 57(4), 657-74. doi: 10.1111/0022-4537.00234
- Heilman, M.E. & Okimoto, T.G. (2007). V.11y are women penalized for success at male tasks?: The implied communality

deficit . .foumlll nf AJ1'liPd Psydwf,>[zy, 92(1), 81-92. doi: 10.1037/0021-9010.92.1.81

- Heilman, M. E.; Wallen, A. S.; Fuchs, D.; & Tamkins, M. M. (2004). Penalties for success: Reactions to women who succeed at male gende1~typed tasks . .fm1mlll of Af1'liRd P•ydwlogy, 89(3), 416--427. doi: 10.1037/0021-9010.89.3.416
- Hoyt, C. (2015). Soci,,/ ihntiliPs find lnu/r1'hifJ: 17.- wsP of gnidn: In G. Goethals, S. Alison, R. Kramer, & D.
- Messick's (Eds.) ConctjJfions of /,nulrnldfJ: Endming Idn« rmd EmPrging iflsights (pp. 71-91). New York,
- NY: Palgrave Macmillan.
- Hoyt, C. L. & Murphy, S. (2016). Managing to clear the air: Stereotype threat, women, and leadership. 77,,, /,nulmhi/1 Q1wrtn1y, 27(3), 387-399. doi:l0.1016/j.leaqua.2015.11.002
- Kellerman, B. & Rhode, D. L. (2007). \Vmnm find IRflrfn,hi/1: 171P Stfllt o{l'lay llnrl Stmtrgiesfor CluwgP. San Francisco, CA: Jossey-Bass.
- Khazan, 0. (2016, February23). The scourge of the female chore burden. TheA1/m1tic. Retrieved from http:/ I www. theatlan tic .com/business/ archive /2016/ 02/ the-scou rge-0f-the-f emale-time-cru nch/ 4 703 79 /
- Koenig, A.; Eagly, A.; Mitchell, A.; & Ristikari, T. (2011). Are leader stereotypes masculine? A meta-analysis of three research paradigms. l\vc/10/111,>im//J111/P1in, /37(4), 616-642. doi:l0.1037/a0023557
- Milkie, M.; Raley, S.; & Bianchi, S. (2009). Taking on the second shift: Time allocations and time pressures of U.S. parents with preschoolers. SociJ1/ forrPs, 88(2), 487-517. doi: I 0.1353/ sof.0.0268

- Paxton, P.; Kunovich, S.; & Hughes, M. M. (2007). Gender in politics. Anmw.l Rrmiew o{SwiJJ/ogy, 33, 263-284, doi:I0.1146/annurev.soc.33.040406.131651
- Powell, G. N. & Graves, L. M. (2003). \\'t111um find mn1 in wmflgnnnit (3rd ed.). Thousand Oaks, CA: Sage.
- Ryan, M. K. et al. (2016). Getting on top of the glass cliff: Reviewing a decade of evidence, explanations, and impact. n., /,mrlershi/1 Q11arlrrly. doi:l0.1016/j.leaqua.2015.10.008
- Schwartz, S. H. & Rubel, T, (2005). Sex differences in value priorities: Cross-cultural and multimethod studies . .foumal of Pmonfllity and SoriJ1l Psydw/11/!)", 89, 1010-1028. doi: 10.1037 /0022-3514.89.6.1010
- Steele, C. M. (1997). A threat in tile air: How stereotypes shape intellectual identity and performance, Amn~ iwn l" Jrl111/11J.,>i.<I, 52(6), 613-629. doi:l0.1037 /0003-066X.52.6.613
- Steele, C.M.; Spencer, SJ.; & Aronson,]. (2002). Contending with group image: The psychology of sterecr type and social identity threat. In M. Zanna (Ed.), Ar/vane~• in exfmimml-fll soci,,/ fJsyrlwlogy (Vol. 34, pp. 379-440). New York, NY: Academic Press.
- Uhlmann, E. L. & Cohen, G. (2005). Constructed criteria: Redefining merit to justify discrimination. Psydw/111,>iml Sdffla, 16(6), 474-480.
- Williams, R. J. (2003). Women on corporate boards of directors and their influence on corporate philanthropy . .f1111rnal 1if / h1.<inr.u Ethirs, 42(I), 1-10. doi:I0.1023/ A:l021626024014
- World Bank. (2012). GPflrln•rq1wlity and drod<1nnml: \forld dnwl11nnn1/ 1"fHn•t, 2012. Washington, DC: International

Bank for Reconstruction and Development, World Bank. Retrieved from http:/ /issuu.com/world.bank.publications/ docs/9780821388105

- The Confidence Effect (a book) Grace Killelea, (2016) pgs. 167-168)
- Black Women are Earning More College degrees, but that alone won't close race gaps (article from the Brookings Institute) Richard V. Reeves and Katherine Guyot – Monday, December 4, 2017
- New Study Shows Black Women are Among the Most Educated Groups in the United States (Essence Magazine) Rachaell Davis October 27, 2020
- Stress and Your Health (US Department of Health & Human Services) June, 2022
- How Janice Bryant Howroyd turned $900 loan from her mom into a billion-dollar business (CNBC, Courtney Connley, April 20, 2018)
- Overcoming Imposter Syndrome, (article) Harvard Business Review by Gill Corkindale, Ma7 7, 2008
- 12 Leaders, Entrepreneurs and Celebrities Who Have struggled with Imposter Syndrome, Entrepreneur.com, Rose Leadem, November 8, 2017
- 5 Different Types of Imposter Syndrome. The Muse by Melody Wilding
- Serena Williams' Husband Alexis on the Importance of Paternity Leave, Essentially Sports, by Samarveer Singh (January 16, 2022)
- Theories of Personality, Simply Psychology by Saul McLeod, 2021
- The Hidden Advantage of Women in Leadership. Inc. Shama

Hyder June 2022

- Ex-Xerox CEO Ursula Burns, CNBC Make It, Courtney Connley, June 17, 2020
- A Review of Prospect Theory, Journal of Human Resources & Sustainability Studies Volume 7 No. 1 March 2019
- The Black Ceiling: Why African American Women Aren't Making It to The Top in Corporate America. Ellen McGirt, Sept 2017 Fortune
- How Women Leaders Impact the Bottom line – Fast Company, Jacqueline Carter, March 22, 2022
- How Dr. Tanjia Coleman is Revolutionizing Diversity and Talent Management, Disrupt Magazine, June 19, 2022 Evan Arroyo
- Are you a Risk Taker, Psychology Today, Marvin Zuckerman, Dec 2019
- Why You Need a Personal Board of Advisors and How To Build One; LinkedIn, July 23, 2021
- Women in the Workplace 2021, Sept 2021 7th year; McKinsey & Company
- Why You Need a Personal Board of Advisors and How To Build One; LinkedIn, July 23, 2021, Elise Awwad
- Sorensen, P.F., Yaeger, T.F. (2017). The Human Side of Douglas McGregor. In: Szabla, D., Pasmore, W., Barnes, M., Gipson, A. (eds) The Palgrave Handbook of Organizational Change Thinkers. Palgrave Macmillan, Cham. doi.org/10.1007/978-3-319-49820-1_18-1

www.ingramcontent.com/pod-product-compliance
Lightning Source LLC
Chambersburg PA
CBHW030519210326
41597CB00013B/964
9780645676587